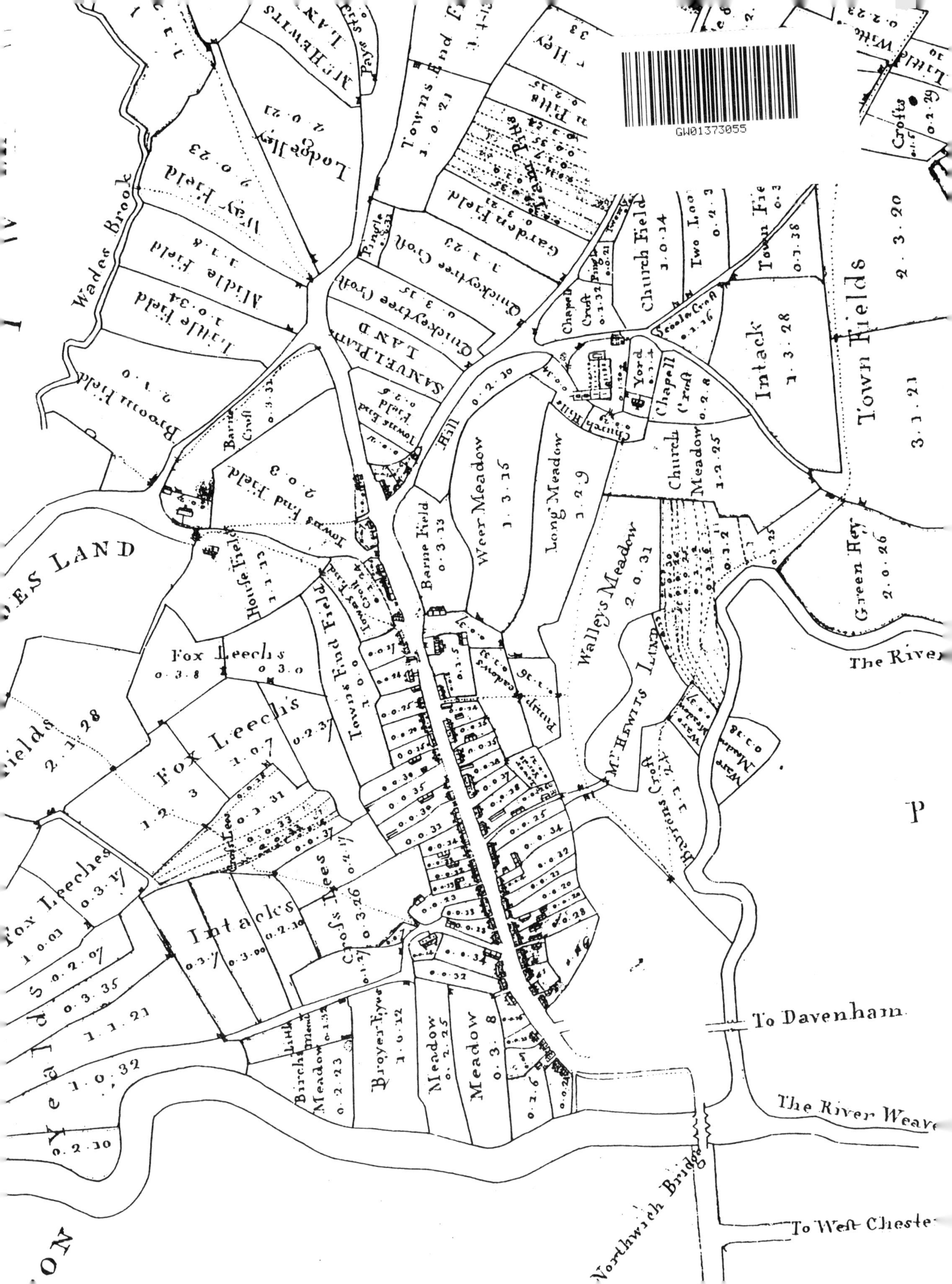

Wades Brook
Way Field 2 0 23
Lodge Hey 2 0 21
Midle Field 1 1 8
Little Field 1 0 34
Broom Field 2 1 0
Towns End Field
Garden Field
Quickeytree Croft
SAMUEL PLATT LAND
Pingle
Barne Croft
Towns End Field 2 0 3
House Field 1 1 13
Fox Leechs 0 3 8
0 3 0
Fox Leech's 1 0 7
0 2 37
Fox Leechs 1 2 3
Fox Leeches 0 3 17
Fox Leeches 1 0 03
Intacks
Cross Lees 0 3 26
Towns End Field 1 0 0
Barne Field 0 3 13
Hill 0 2 10
Weer Meadow 1 3 15
Long Meadow 1 2 9
Church Field 1 0 14
Chapell Croft
Yord
Chapell Croft 0 2 8
Church Hill
Church Meadow 1 2 25
Walleys Meadow 2 0 31
Intack 1 3 28
Town Fields 2 3 20
Town Fields 3 1 21
Town Field 0 1 38
Two L
Scoole Croft 0 1 26
Green Hey 2 0 26
Mr. Hewits Land
Burrows Croft
Ware Meadow 0 3 38
Birch Meadow 0 2 23
Broyer Eyes 1 0 12
Meadow 0 2 25
Meadow 0 3 8
ES LAND
ields 2 1 28
The River
P
To Davenham
The River Weave
Northwich Bridge
To West Cheste
ON

THE BOOK OF NORTHWICH & DISTRICT

FRONT COVER: The floods of 1872 in Witton Street. Life went on as normal, milk was delivered from a churn on a raft via a jug on a string, men were hired to carry people through the water and boats delivered supplies. (ICI)

ABOVE: Castle Street subsidence and BELOW: The unofficial badge used by the Urban District Council until 1962, the Rural District Council Arms and the arms granted to the Urban District Council in 1962, now used by the Town Council.

THE BOOK OF NORTHWICH & DISTRICT

BY

J. BRIAN CURZON
BA MA (Manc) MA (Leics) AMA.

SAL EST VITA (salt is life)
— Town Council motto

BARON
MCMXCIII

PUBLISHED BY BARON BIRCH
FOR QUOTES LIMITED
AND PRODUCED BY KEY COMPOSITION,
SOUTH MIDLANDS LITHOPLATES, CHENEY & SONS LTD,
HILLMAN (PRINTERS) LIMITED AND
WBC BOOKBINDERS LTD

© J. Brian Curzon 1993

All rights reserved. No part of this publication may be reproduced, stored in a retrieval system, or transmitted, in any form or by any means, electronic, mechanical, photocopying, recording or otherwise, without the prior permission of Quotes Limited.

Any copy of this book issued by the Publisher as clothbound or as a paperback is sold subject to the condition that it shall not by way of trade or otherwise, be lent, re-sold, hired out or otherwise circulated without the Publisher's prior consent, in any form of binding or cover other than that in which it is published, and without a similar condition including this condition being imposed on a subsequent purchaser.

ISBN 0 86023 519 X

Contents

Acknowledgements	8
Foreword by County Cllr Ron Carey, Deputy Lieutenant	9
Introduction	11
Off the Record	12
Roman Condate	16
In the Royal Manor	22
A Pretty Towne, But Fowled	26
Parliamentary Stronghold	31
Beacon of the Industrial Revolution	35
A Smoking Hell Hole	40
For Righteousness' Sake	50
An Inland Port	55
The Curse of the Country	73
Pioneering Partners: Brunner Mond	88
White Slaves and Other Workers	93
Repaying the Community	100
One of England's Curiosities	112
In Search of Paradise	126
Bloodsports To Beatles	135
They Changed Our Llives	148
Postscript	153
Bibliography	154
Index	156
Subscribers	160

Acknowledgements

I would like to thank Councillor Colin Lynch, whose books of pictures of Old Northwich have delighted many, for reading my original draft. Professor Barri Jones has helped with information on the Roman period on which new light is cast every time he digs on Castle. Andrew Bowan, Editor of the *Northwich Chronicle*, allowed access to their files for many illustrations. Lillian Hartley provided much information on Hartford. Needless to say thanks are also due to those who have loaned precious pictures for illustrations. Sheilagh Scragg and the Staff at Northwich Library allowed special access to the local history collection and the staff at Winsford Library also allowed access to books which were more convenient to use. Stephen Pardoe took some photos specially for the book and copied others for it. Nick Hughes and the DAN organisation have made the production of the book easier in many ways. The Market Place Column of the *Northwich Guardian,* always a source of memoirs, published useful appeals for information and illustrations. My thanks are due to many others past and present who have helped with my researches into Northwich history and who have answered inumerable questions.

This book has been published with financial help from ICI PLC, Brunner Mond PLC and Frank Roberts & Sons.

Key to Caption Credits

AH	Alan Horner for Northwich Archaeology Group	GFB	G. F. Benyon
AM	Ashmolean Museum, Oxford	ICI	ICI Archives
BB	Brian Broadhurst	JC	James Conboy
BCB	Cheshire Brine Compensation Board	JGS	J. Geofrey Sharps
CL	Cheshire Libraries	LS	Lion Salt Works
CJL	Colin Lynch	MH	Margaret Hodgkison
CM	Cheshire Museums Service	NC	Northwich Chronicle
DAN	The Development of Arts in Northwich	NCSW	New Cheshire Salt Works
DG	Derek Gibson	NT	National Trust
GDBJ	Professor G. D. B. Jones, Manchester Univeristy	SP	Stephen Pardoe
		TC	J. A. Curzon

Other photos provided by the author or loaned anonymously.

Foreword

by County Councillor Ron Carey BEM DL, Deputy-Lieutenant of Cheshire

Having represented Northwich as a Councillor since 1968, what a privilege and pleasure it is to contribute to *The Book of Northwich*.

The town has been able to retain many of its uniuque 19th century black and white timber-framed buildings and is a centre for shoppers from a wide surrounding area.

Northwich, in the heart of Cheshire, was in Roman times a military station and then became famous for its salt-making, which has also passed into history, recorded in its unique Salt Museum.

I have known Mr Brian Curzon for many years and acknowlege his contribution to so many aspects of life in Northwich, especially his pioneering work in starting the excavations on the Roman site on Castle Hill and reviving the Salt Museum after years of neglect. His writings in the *Chronicle* and elsewhere have fascinated many. Who better could record the history of this interesting town for the first time?

Dedication

To the staff at the Dialysis Unit, Withington Hospital and the Kidney Transplant Unit at Manchester Royal infirmary; without them I would not be alive today.

> Our Wiches with their plenteous store,
> Of rock salt and of brine,
> I sing a song unsung before,
> By any lyre but mine.

Rowland Egerton Warburton of Arley

Northwich is twinned with Dole in France and Carpow in the Republic of Ireland.

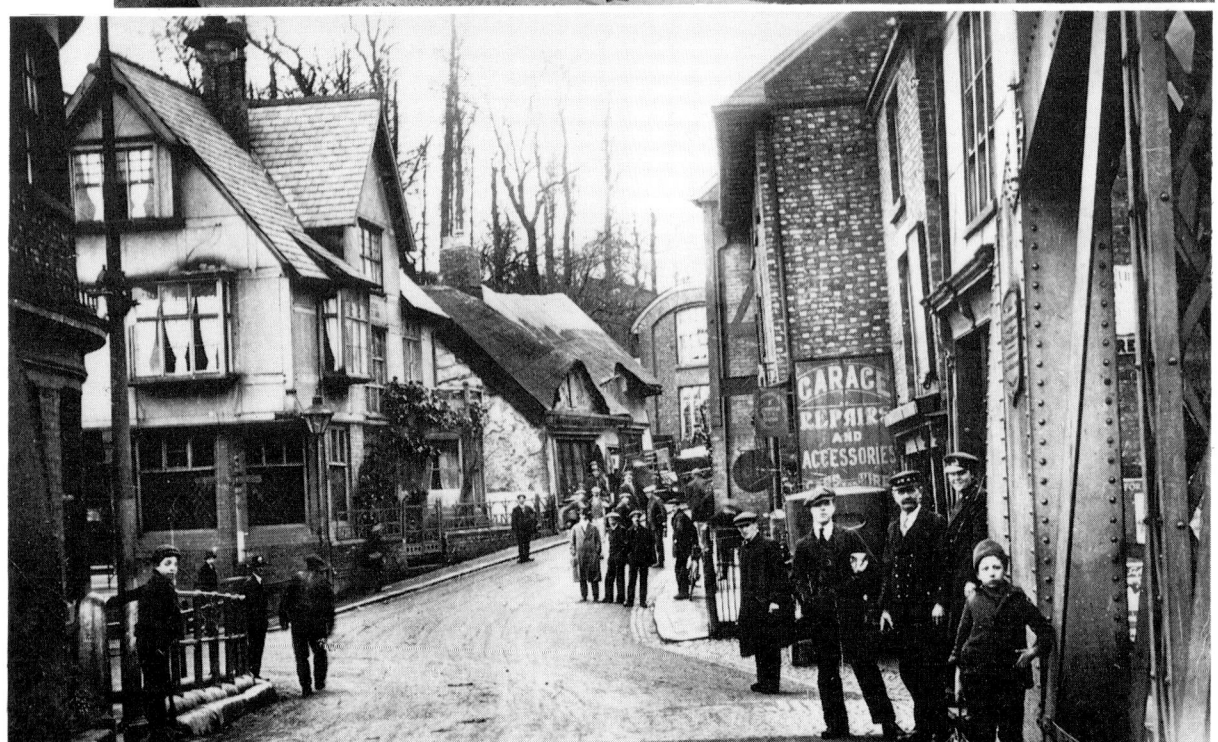

ABOVE: Witton Street 1904, and BELOW: Winnington Hill c1910.

Introduction

The author of a companion volume commented that nothing of national interest took place in Buxton. In contrast I sometimes wished that *less* had taken place here as I researched this book! Northwich was seldom a quiet back-water but a place where things occurred which changed our way of life. Its salt trade established Liverpool as a major port as part of the slave trade and pioneered the transport revolution. The canal age and the Manchester Ship Canal were inspired by developments here. Work here during two World Wars helped to change post-war life. Polythene, nuclear power, artificial fertilizers, jet engines, breeze blocks, and Beatlemania all had their origins here. The list of 'one of the first' seems endless. It includes two Methodist denominations, electric swing-bridges, boat-lifts, fairgrounds, football, industrial museums, village libraries, railways and the communication chain. The index is sprinkled with distinguished names who changed history and the town was known as 'one of the most curious in the land'.

One book can serve as little more than an introduction to the story of the district. Most of the chapters deserve a book to themselves and each one is nothing more than a short essay on the topic. Often a sentence or two summarises a story worthy of a book and many interesting items have had to be missed out altogether. This, the first history of Northwich, has been prepared with particular attention to the needs of students and pupils preparing projects for examinations.

Our idea of the extent of Northwich is only a century old. The creation of the Urban District Council formed a single town known as Northwich in 1894. That area contained several ancient manors. Most was part of Great Budworth Parish but the township of Leftwich (a name derived from a Saxon lady: *Leoftaet's Wich*) in Davenham parish extended right up to the Dane.

Even more confusing, the division of the country into 'hundreds' (areas of 100 settlements) in Saxon times used different boundaries. The Northwich Hundred extends from Wade Brook to the Staffordshire border. Castle and the area to the west of the Weaver is the Eddisbury Hundred, while part of Winnington is in Bucklow. Research into early Northwich means consulting records under all these headings.

It is an exciting and fascinating tale of innovation and resistance to change, of great wealth and abject poverty and above all of hard work.

The town as we know it today was a result of developments in the 1960s; few buildings in the main streets are even 100 years old. Yet it is the successor to an Industrial Revolution boom town, mediaeval manors, Saxon settlements and a Roman fort, with evidence of occupation before that.

ABOVE: The meandering River Dane south of Danefields estate with the railway line to Sandbach. (AH) BELOW: The viaduct of what was known as the Cheshire Midland Railway above Hunts Lock. (AH)

Off the record

The wealth of Mid-Cheshire was built on its salt, chemical and dairy trades which depended on beds of rock salt under the ground.

Their origins go back 250 million years to the Triassic period. Opinions differ slightly on how the salt was formed; some favour the idea of a shallow inland sea, like the Dead Sea. Others prefer the theory of a coastal bay cut off by sand-bars.

Whatever the nature of the water it is clear that rivers and/or tides continually replenished the supply while the climate was exceptionally hot. The rate of evaporation exceeded the rate at which water was replaced, forming a deep bed of almost pure salt. Occasionally floods rushed in, carrying sand and silt, forming patches of organge, red, brown and yellow in the salt which is otherwise clear and crystal-like.

Eventually, because of climatic changes, the supply of water dried up and the sea slowly became desert. For millions of years the sand built up dunes, forming a bed of marl. Then the sea returned to form the upper bed of salt, until conditions for the formation of marl returned. We know nothing of what happened during subsequent millennia until the Ice Age 10 thousand years ago, because ice sheets scoured away the intermediate geological record.

Melting ice deposited boulder clay, full of boulders and cobbles. The ice ground away rocks where ice sheets formed in the Lake District and Scotland, carrying pieces of stone which knocked against each other as it moved, breaking and grinding them down. Cobbles, rounded and polished by the ice, still form a few local pavements. Large boulders (erratics) can be seen by the corners of old buildings, to prevent cart wheels bumping them. The tooth of a mammoth in the old Salt Museum was found in Witton Street.

The ice sheets also left large areas of fine grained sands, (exploited commercially at Sandiway) formed by rapid melting. In hot weather water flowed out quickly, carrying sand but not heavy stones. Known as 'current bedded sands', they consist of thin layers left by successive melts.

The river pattern was formed after the ice melted. The last forward push of ice formed low hills on the Shropshire border. The River Weaver flows south from its source in the Peckforton Hills until the hills force it to turn north.

The dominant winds are warm, humid south-westerlies. Much moisture is lost over the Welsh mountains, causing cloudy skies but reducing heavy rain. In the summer warm air holds more moisture so that May and June are hot and dry while August is often the wettest month. Early sun is good for hay, but not cereals which can be ruined by a wet August. Cheshire specialised in cheese as its cash crop. Shielded from the cold east winds of winter by the Derbyshire hills, Northwich escapes extremes of climate.

Water seeped through the clay onto the top bed of rock salt, dissolving it to form a solution called brine. It often ran over the surface of the rock salt as streams of 'wild brine' which provided the raw material for the salt industry.

From the 18th century, pools were created as a result of industrial brine extraction. Pools made in this way are called 'flashes'. The word is old English for flooded grassland and is also used for collapsed mines in south Lancashire. It is probable that Budworth Mere and Pickmere were formed by natural seepage.

Little is known about prehistoric occupation in the area. A Neolithic polished axe from Coggshall and a Bronze Age stone axe-hammer found near Sir John Deane's College indicate tree felling for agriculture. A few worked flints were found on Castle, including a fine thumb scraper sharp enough to cut paper like a razor. Several flint implements found around Lostock, including a beautifully worked flint hand hammer, are mentioned in the church history.

A prehistoric route along which stone axes were traded down the Dane to the Trent Valley and the Weaver to the Severn has been suggested.

The mound where Roman burials were found on Winnington Hill could have been a Bronze Age round barrow, as Romans sometimes buried their dead in existing barrows. Two mounds which some believed were remains of a castle on Castle were described by a writer in 1900 as burial mounds and Gibbet Hill at Hartford was also a barrow.

No finds from the (Celtic) Iron Age have come to light. It is claimed that the Romans found the natives made salt by pouring brine onto hot stones but the only record of this is from Spain. River names have Celtic origins, such as Weaver for a winding river. The Dane or Daven reflects the name of the Celtic river goddess, found in a variety of river-names including Deva, Dee, Don, Danube etc. The Peover Eye is Celtic for a sparkling stream.

Until comparatively recently the area was thickly forested with peat bogs and swampy valleys likely to flood, which did not attract settlers.

Great Budworth's mediaeval village plan, garden plots behind the houses enclosed by the village ditch. The Roman road passes between the village and Mere. (AH)

The town centre 1974. The gas tower, Witton Albion ground and Bus Terminus have since disappeared. (AH)

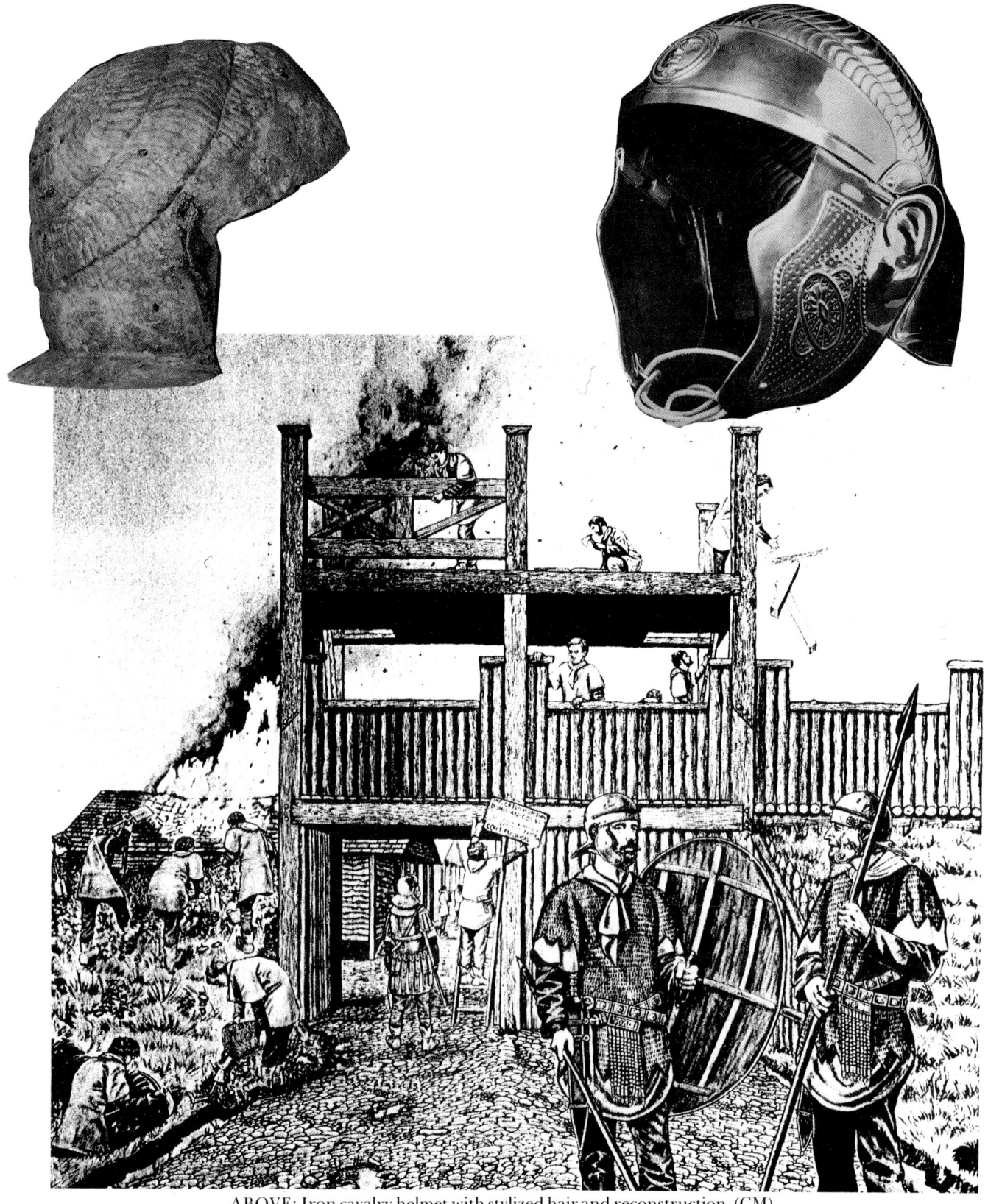

ABOVE: Iron cavalry helmet with stylized hair and reconstruction. (CM)
BELOW: The first Roman fort was systematically taken apart to prevent hostile natives using it. (GDBJ)

Roman Condate

Was there a castle on Castle? The evidence is uncertain, worsened by changes to landscape caused by subsidence and building. 'Banks and ditches' and 'two mounts of unequal height', one 90 feet in diameter, were described by 19th century writers. The site is marked on early OS maps in Verdin Park above the concrete retaining wall, now levelled for gardens. Writers misled by the name 'Castle' suggested that they were remains of a Norman motte and bailey. There is no record of any such structure and 90 feet is too small for a motte. The earliest mention of 'Castle' is in 1189 and was used for the area, not a building.

Its likely origin is from the Latin *Castra* or fort. Manchester's Castlefields, and Castleshaw near Huddersfield on the same road to York have similar origins. There is certainly evidence of two phases of Roman forts but none (at present) of later fortifications or occupation.

Knowledge of Roman Northwich has advanced since 1967 as a result of rescue excavations but any account must come from current archaeological evidence.

Roman occupation of high land west of the Weaver valley started in the '70s of the first century AD when a timber auxiliary fort was established. Weaver Street and the road into Verdin Park have streams culverted under them, whose valleys added to the defences of the site. The stream under Verdin Park was Lamprey Brook, mentioned in old records as the boundary between Northwich and Castle.

The road from Chester to York crossed the Weaver where it was joined by the Dane. Sand banks built up as the water slowed; today a dredger is needed to keep the channel clear. The 1721 Weaver Navigation Act stated the water was only 3ft deep at Northwich Bridge. A ford would be passable in summer, but a timber bridge was probably needed as the river was liable to flood. The name *condate* (confluence), now identified with Northwich, might indicate worship of the Celtic god Condatis; guardian of waters-meeting. It was customary to pray to the water spirits before crossing.

Settlement can be inferred from the historical record given by Tacitus in his account of General Agricola. In the '50s the Romans established peace with the state of Brigantia (now Lancashire and Yorkshire). Tacitus tells how Cartimandua, Queen of Brigantia, left her consort for his armour bearer in 60 AD. Her pro-Roman policy upset many of her subjects, who followed the consort in rebellion. She asked her Roman allies for support. Under the Governor Cerialis, Agricola led the 20th Legion, probably from Chester through Northwich and Manchester. Tacitus records soldiers complaining about cold wet weather, swampy ground and unpleasant natives. Cartimandua was rescued but Brigantia remained independent until 78 AD when, as Governor, Agricola used the same road to extend Roman rule to Carlisle, then into Scotland.

Agricola was responsible for founding over 70 forts and building 2,100 kilometres of roads. A military road with forts at intervals of a day's march along it was typical of the frontiers established by Agricola as he pushed northwards. York was founded in 71 and it is likely that the line of forts was established around the same date to contain the Brigantians. The road from Dover through London and Chester to York is listed in the Antonine Itinerary of the 4th Century (Iter II) recording the name *condate* (pronounced con-dar-tay). It was believed that Northwich was called *Salinae* (salt pits), but this is now attributed to Middlewich.

King Street, from Middlewich to Broken Cross (the modern road above the Roman), appears to have been built around 90 AD. It was a military supply route to the north. The date evidence comes from bright red, factory-made pottery called Samian ware. It was made to designs which varied over the years and have been classified into 'forms'. An angular bowl (form 29), was out of fashion by 80 AD. It was found on Castle, giving evidence of the date but not at Wilderspool and Middlewich on King Street. The fact that this main arterial road by-passed Northwich suggests that the fort was obsolete when it was built. A group of bowl fragments was identified from the same pottery factory (probably of *Mercato*) which must have been sent from France soon after the fort was founded.

Excavations on Castle before rebuilding revealed traces of timber barrack buildings and the surrounding defensive ditch with a turf rampart faced with timber.

The Chester Road formed the main street (*Via Principalis*) of the fort. It was occupied by a (so far) unknown auxiliary regiment. Flanking Waterloo Road, there appears to have been a fortified annexe for industrial production.

The fort was abandoned in the '80s as Agricola' pushed into Scotland. It was re-occupied after 120 when Hadrian reorganised military occupation in the north, centred on his wall. The gate-towers and rampart-facing were rebuilt of stone. This was reduced in size and, perhaps, finally abandoned when Antoninus Pius constructed a new frontier further north after 143. A spear-head found in the corner of a barracks might have been left inside as they were systematically demolished. The Freemason's Arms is in a 19th century cutting below the level of the east gate. Stones from it were probably re-used for the adjoining retaining wall. Victorian accounts of 'a great foundation' could have been the gate, unearthed when the road (known as the Hollow Way) was lowered. The site was abandoned by the end of the 2nd century. Probably settlement then centred around the river crossing.

In the period between the military occupations, around 100 AD, native civilians occupied the military site, undertaking a variety of industrial processes. A kiln was operated by a potter who stamped his name *Maco* on his wares. Several furnaces and smithing hearths were found which were used for shaping iron. A damaged iron auxiliary helmet was buried with cheek pieces from two other helmets, suggesting it awaited repair. This is similar to an armourer's chest, buried at Chester. Northwich, Middlewich and Wilderspool served as supply bases for the military to the north. Cheshire has been termed the Roman Black Country.

The discovery of a fragment of lead salt pan in the Roman ditch confirms that four pans with cast inscriptions found by workmen digging a dock in 1864 were Roman. The fragment has the name of the owner, *Veluvius*, cast into it in letters identical to the others. They match letters on pig-lead and on lead water pipes from Chester, while the techniques of casting and shaping is identical to other Roman lead objects such as a coffin from Warrington. Lead was in ready supply for pan-making. Welsh lead ores were exploited in the '70s for their silver content. Tests on the pans showed silver had been extracted from the lead. Both silver and salt were needed to pay soldiers; the latter for the *Salarium* (salt pay; hence salary).

It is tempting to think that a 'pig' of lead found near Chester, by the road to Northwich, fell from a cart *en route*. A find of twenty 'pigs' from the Mersey at Runcorn suggests that lead (and building stone) were transported by water. The pan fragment from Castle and a complete pan marked *III* are on display in the Salt Museum. Pieces of two pans, marked

IIICCCIII and *DEVE*, went to Warrington Museum. The rest were destroyed by their discoverers for scrap.

Other areas of occupation are difficult to identify. Tacitus says Agricola's forts 'were protected against long protracted siege by supplies renewed every year'. There must have been extensive farming to supply it. When Hartford Station was built in 1837 two burial urns were found which are in Warrington Museum, one containing cremated ashes. The pottery was made in Northwich Kilns around 100 AD. They might indicate a farm in that area. (A lead spindle whorl found in Stones Manor Lane is mediaeval). Roman burial urns were found in a mound levelled when Winnington Lodge (then Oakleigh) was built. One is a kiln-waster from a local kiln and is in the Grosvenor Museum.

The place-name Wallerscote could indicate a Romano-British settlement. *Waller* was the Saxon word for the Romanised Britons (meaning 'foreigner', as in Wallasey) while *cote* is Saxon for dwelling. Alternatively *waller* might be a salt-maker. A section of Roman road, said to have been discovered in Weaverham church-yard, is difficult to relate to any known Roman route. In 1970 a fragment of a 2nd century Samian plate was found near Waterloo Road with a scratched mark on the base. This appeared to be a 'Chi-rho' (early Christian secret sign made by crossing P and X). This was earlier than any other Christian find from Britain, and was difficult to accept until a Christian word-square of similar date was found in Manchester. This suggests that the plate was used for communion services in Northwich within a century of the Last Supper.

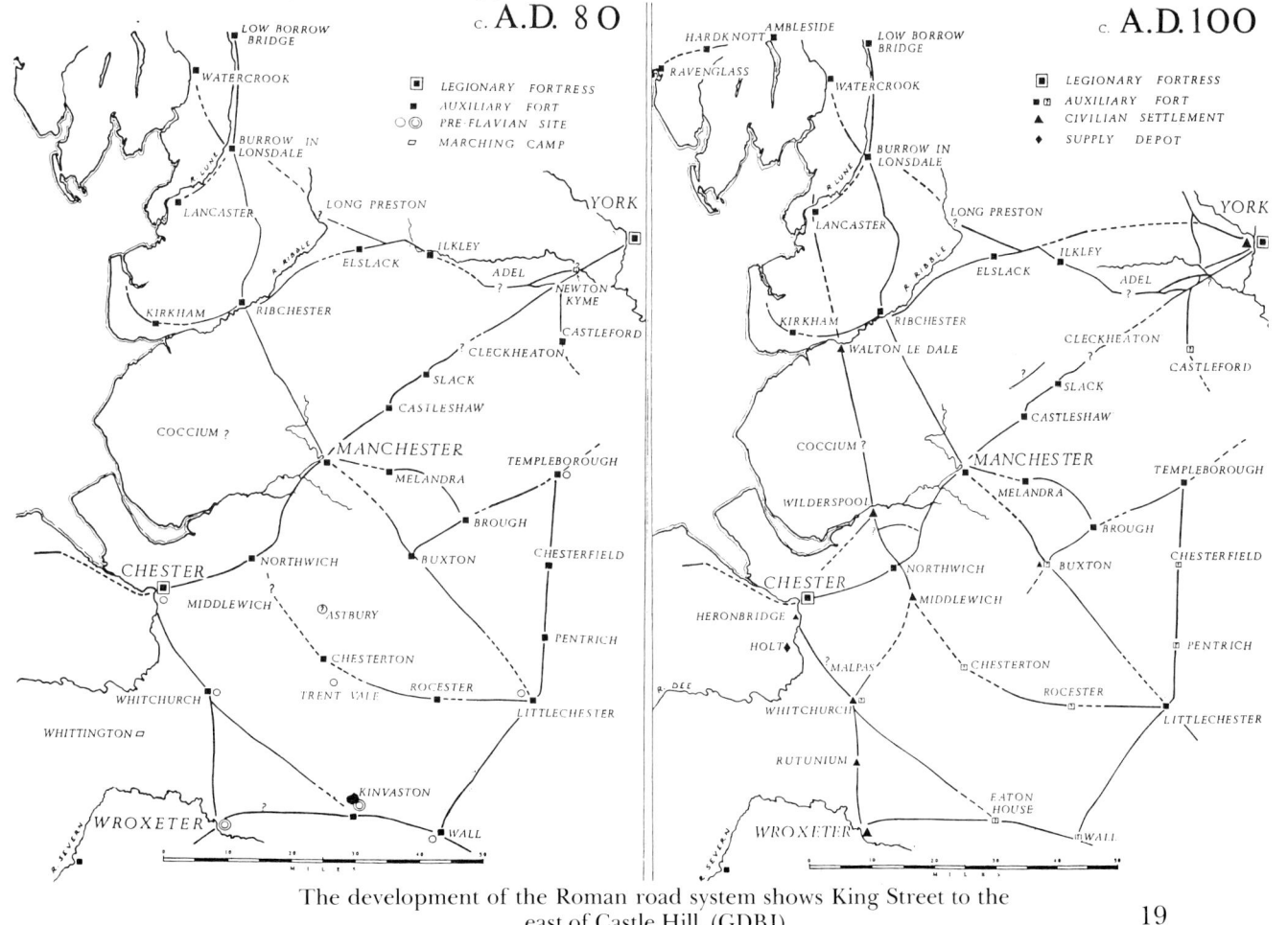

The development of the Roman road system shows King Street to the east of Castle Hill. (GDBJ)

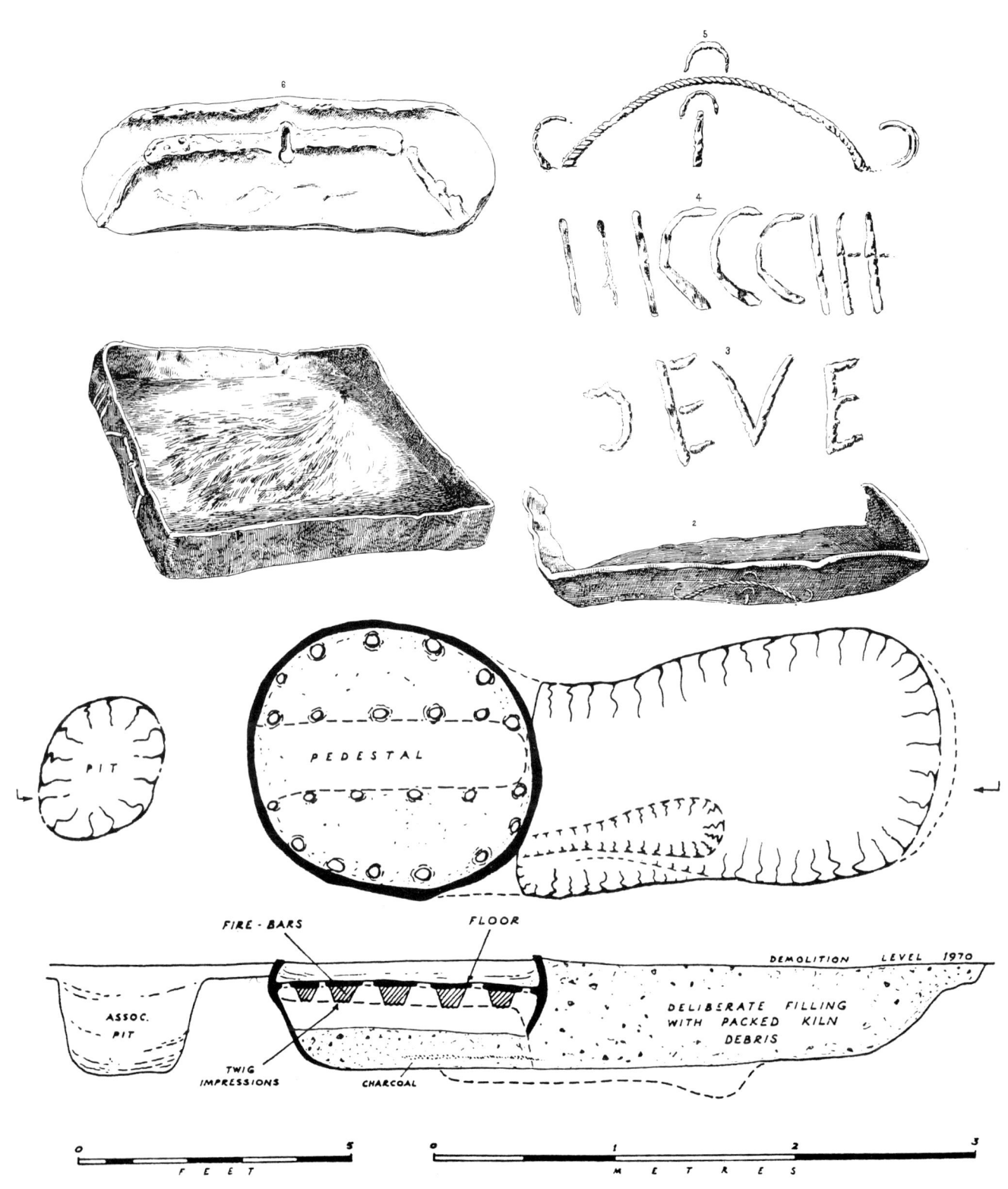

ABOVE: Roman lead salt pan and fragments found in 1864. BELOW:
Plan and section of the pottery kiln.

LEFT: Roman salt pan (top). The smaller pan, (from Ashton's Works) is the size specified in the Domesday Book. (ICI) RIGHT: The dark profile of the filled-in north defensive ditch. (GDBJ) BELOW: The site of the Roman fort with the military road, 1967. (GDBJ)

ABOVE: Witton Church with the second Grammar School building 1794, and LEFT: before 1886, when galleries were removed from the aisles and the pulpit was sold to Barnton. RIGHT: This Victorian print shows the apse-like east end.

22

In the Royal Manor

There is no record of what happened in Northwich for 800 years after the Romans left Castle. There is no archaeological evidence, for the area that had been settled was wrecked by salt subsidence. The names *Halath Wen* (white salt town) for Nantwich and *Halath Ddu* (black — or darker — salt town) for Northwich mentioned in Camden's *Britannia* (1586) are Welsh names. It has been suggested that they were used in the Dark Ages or earlier but it is more likely that they were used by Welsh traders. An extensive network of routes into Wales and Derbyshire has been identified from place-names such as Salterswall and Saltersford. The trade was so important that during the Welsh wars Henry III ordered the salt wells (more likely the roads to them) to be stopped to cut off Welsh supplies.

Place name elements such as *ton* and *ham* indicate Saxon origins for most of the villages. The suffix *wich* has traditionally been associated with salt-making; recent suggestions that it derives from the Latin *vicus* (small town) also apply to the three 'wiches'.

During the 8th century pagan Danish settlers pushed from Yorkshire into Cheshire. The Saxon Queen Ethelflaeda established defences around 910 AD. There is no evidence for suggestions that she erected a fortification on Castle but large parishes in West Cheshire may represent 10th century conversion of the Danish lands. Modern Northwich was split between Great Budworth (the second largest parish in England) and Davenham parishes. Budworth was 10 miles long and five miles wide. It was never convenient for all parishioners to attend services there. In the 17th century Adam Martindale wrote 'the minister of Great Budworth and I had such vast parishes that multitudes of the people would be dead, in all probability, ere we could goe over them once'. From Norman times Budworth belonged to Norton Priory, who appointed the priests and took the tythes.

The manor of Northwich (eight acres at the confluence) belonged to the Earls of Chester until the last died in 1237. Wallerscote and Northwich passed into the possession of Prince Edward, son of Henry III, becoming Royal manors from 1257 when he was made Earl of Chester. In 1277, as King Edward I, he laid the foundation stone of Vale Royal Abbey, staying at Wallerscote with his Queen, courtiers, servants and soldiers. King Edward was in the district again in 1292, granting the market charter for Knutsford at 'Hartford' — probably Wallerscote. Northwich beloned to a Prince of Wales for most of the next 300 years. It was usually 'farmed' to noble families, who collected the tolls in exchange for a set rental.

The salt-makers — and others — lived in the area along the Roman Road known as *Wich Tune* (Witton) — 'The town at the wich'. This was part of the barony of Kinderton belonging to the Venables family, kinsmen of the Conqueror. Ribbon development took place, with houses set in burgage plots. The street frontage was the width of a good beam (15 feet) with gardens for vegetables and enclosures for animals behind. The arrangement of shop fronts along Witton Street today preserves the width of the old plots or multiples of them.

Witton absorbed Twambrooks, (between Witton and Wade Brookes) by 1430, becoming Witton cum Twambrooks.

The tiny manor of Le Cross may have taken its name from a Saxon preaching cross; it became a market centre, giving the name Cross Street near the modern market. When a place of worship was established in Witton is uncertain but the dedication to St Helen close to a Roman site suggests an early foundation. As mother of Constantine she was popular in late Roman times. The earliest known structure is the 14th century south colonnade. A gravestone of that date, found during Victorian alterations, was broken to remove it. Underneath, in a stone coffin, was the perfectly preserved body of a priest in vestments, which disintegrated when exposed to the air.

Enlargements started in the late 15th century, and continued for about 50 years. Richard Wynington left 40 shillings towards 'making the steeple' in 1498. In 1525 Randle Pickmere of Middlewich left 20 shillings to 'the blessed seynt elyn of Witton and her churchwerke'. It is said that Thomas Hunter, whose name is on the tower, was the master-mason also responsible for the tower at Great Budworth. However, during alterations, inscriptions were moved around fairly liberally. Stones bearing an inscription were reused in various parts of the porch; it translates as 'Richard Alkoke Chaplain, Clerk of works'. Alkoke was active around 1460. Inside the Belfry is another inscribed stone with the name 'Johannes' (John). The window at the east of the south aisle was, apparently, the original main east window, removed, turned round and rebuilt to save a stained glass memorial window. The apsidal east end resembles the old Coventry Cathedral — which was claimed to be unique.

Tradition claimed the church was widened because the timber ceiling was moved from Norton Priory at the Dissolution. Excavations at Norton proved that the church there was 10 feet narrower than the ceiling at Witton and the same width as Witton before enlargement. There is ample proof in the ceiling bosses that it was made for Witton, including representations of salt 'barrows' — conical baskets used to drain salt — and the initials of William Venables, Lord of the Manor.

The salt industry was well organised by 1086 when Domesday Book recorded the taxes forming an important part of the revenue of Hugh Lupus, Earl of Chester as Lord of the Manor of Northwich. It was similar to an industrial estate, with numerous small salt houses. The account was only concerned with the taxes and the fines which were set on those who tried to evade them. Overloading a pack-horse to break its back or loading a cart so that the axle broke brought fines of two shillings if taken within the league but nothing beyond. A small lead salt pan found near Ashton's Salt Works (now in the Salt Museum) holds the same quantity of brine as specified in Domesday.

A tax of 4d was paid by each ox-cart from another shire, but only 2d from Cheshire, if it was for 'own use'. If it was not paid within three nights of returning home a fine of 40 shillings was due. Carters living in the hundred who took salt to sell paid 1d a cart-load in tax. Pack-horses were charged 1d if they came from outside the county but only one farthing if not. Those selling salt from pack-horses were charged 1d, to be paid at Martinmas. Before 1066 Northwich was valued at £8 and the revenue was shared between Edward the Confessor and Earl Edwin of Chester. In 1086 its value was reduced to 35 shillings. This was the result of resistance to the Norman Conquest, suppressed in 1068 when much of Cheshire was laid waste. The area of the wich was exempt from normal law. Apart from murder or crimes deserving the death penalty all other crimes were fined two shillings or 30 boilings of salt. Salt made each Friday was tax-free.

There is no evidence of a castle on Castle or of occupation there. Preferential tax consideration given to people form the Northwich hundred in salt making and trade would make people reluctant to live there, as Castle was in Eddisbury Hundred.

The exact status of Northwich is uncertain. No charter is known, but in Edward I's inquest into military service of 1288, Northwich is recorded as a 'borough', required to supply 12 foot soldiers for the Welsh wars. A charter was required to allow a market and a weekly market was held in the manor of Cross.

Extending from the east of Witton towards Holmes Chapel, Rudheath Lordship was a large sandy heath and a Royal demesne which became a criminals sanctuary. At Rudheath was the manor of Drakelow; the name refers to a legendary dragon guarding treasure in a prehistoric burial mound. No trace of the mound (or dragon!) survives.

Northwich Bridge occurs in documents when floods damaged it. A small part of Northwich manor extended to the foot of Winnington Hill, enclosing the whole bridge in one township, hence 'Town Bridge'. As boundaries followed rivers, most bridges were the joint responsibility of townships, causing disputes about responsibility for repairs. As a Royal possession, records of Northwich Bridge are particularly detailed.

In 1351 an inquisition before the Justice of Chester was told that Northwich Bridge had fallen down owing to the floods and 'if it was not repaired the Prince [of Wales] would suffer loss'. Pontage (tax to use the bridge) was allowed at 4d for a cart, 2d for a loaded horse and 1d for a man carrying goods.

In 1353 a long list of tolls for everything crossing the bridge was approved. This did not include fuel, or salt, which was taxed at the salt-house. It did include carcases of ox or cow; fleeces; hides of horse, mare or bull; skins of lambs, kids, hares, rabbits, foxes, cats and squirrels; herrings, large fish, eels, lamprey and salmon; wine, cider and mead; cloth, canvas, worsted, tapestry and silk; iron, pitch, resin or tallow; fat, butter or cheese; onion seeds; shingles, timber, bark, roof nails; other nails; horseshoes; wooden dishes and platters (charged by the thousand); tin, copper, brass, lead; hemp and flax, jars of oil or salted herrings; coloured and white glass and even millstones.

By 1391 damage to the bridge had again occurred and a warrant was issued, requiring John Done, Forester of Delamere, to provide timber for repairs carried out by William Newhall, the King's Carpenter. In 1488 the bridge was again damaged by floods.

Fishing from the Weaver was organised; in 1337 John le Fysser (the fisher) rented the weirs at Wallerscote and Saltersford. He set eel traps on them and was required to give '48 strikes of eels and 12 large eels' to Vale Royal Abbey, which controlled that part of the river. In 1320 the Abbot paid to repair Winnington Bridge. Salmon were taken from the Weaver and Dane until the construction of locks in 1721 stopped them swimming upstream.

ABOVE: Holford Hall, Plumley, with two unconnected wings; it was proposed to fill the moat with lime waste in the 1930s! BELOW: Leftwich Hall; the tower appears to be a pele tower and the cupola might have been a louvre over an open hearth. (CL)

A Pretty Towne, But Fowled

Around 1650 John Leyland described Northwich as 'a pretty towne but fowled by the smoke of many salt houses'. A manuscript written by W. Leftwich in 1593 starts:

'There is and hath been time out of mind within the towne of Northwich ffivescore and Twelve, ffour Leades, and One odd Leade and no more, but four leades of wallinge called the Riminge Wich house. So the total sum is ffivescore and Thirteen four Leades and one odd Leade, which stand in Town rowe, as followeth.'

The account lists the owners of each salt house, most of which contained four rectangular lead salt-pans, though ten contained six. Most houses belonged to local gentry. Abbeys had owned salt houses which passed into private hands and Sir John Deane left one such to provide funding for his school. Wealthy owners hired workers who were allocated pans and provided with fuel and brine. They did not receive wages but the owners purchased the salt produced.

One six-pan salt house called 'The Rimming House' provided salt for Lord Derby's kitchen. Henry VII made Thomas Stanley Earl of Derby as a reward for his part at Bosworth Field. Richard III gave Northwich to Stanley as one of the gifts with which he hoped to buy loyalty in 1484, following the death of Edward, Prince of Wales. Shakespeare tells how Stanley stood to one side during the Battle of Bosworth, until he was sure Richard was defeated, then took his forces to support Henry VII, symbolically giving him the crown after the battle. With this the Middle Ages came to an end. Stanley had married Henry's widowed mother, who had been implicated in a rebellion, and his brother had been declared a traitor but Richard held his son (Lord L'Estrange) as a hostage. Stanley took men from his estates (including Northwich?) to the battle. In 1495 Henry stayed at Vale Royal with his Queen as a guest of the Abbot, on his way to a grand reception at Stanley's Lathom Hall in Lancashire.

The salt-making area, Northwich Manor, stretched from Town Bridge to Boundary Street; it was just eight acres until extended to The Cut after 1784. High Street was called Town Row; the Seath (corrupted to Sheath) Street ran parallel to the Dane. (Its name and Watling Street were used for roads on new sites in the 1960s.) Sheath Street and the brine pit known as 'Brine-seath' derive from *seething* (boiling). Next to this were Yate Street, Leach Eye and Leach End (also called Bakehouse Street). It contained the bakehouse owned by Lord Derby, where all bread was baked. There was a leadsmithy where the pans were repaired. The 'Lodporne Stone' was a landmark, probably corrupted from 'lead-pan'. It might have been used to measure pans.

Two acres close to the salt houses were known as 'Crum Hills' or 'Crymes Heath'. They were areas where impurities from the salt boiling and other waste were tipped. Rules passed in the Manorial Court forbade dunghills and swine-cotes to face the street. A passage of a yard and a half between the house front and the crest of the road had to be kept clear of rubbish, goods and wood-piles to let traffic past. Large animals were forbidden to go loose in the streets as they damaged the salt-houses and brine channels. Such matters only went to court when they became intolerable nuisances.

The salt pit was close to the River Dane. Men stripped to the waist hauled the brine from the depths, passing leather buckets from hand to hand, pouring it into channels along which it ran to the salt houses. Brine was stored in casks sunk into the ground. Boiling times were strictly limited and a bell was rung to indicate when to light the fires. The wich houses were the prerogative of women called 'wallers', from the Saxon word *weallan*, meaning to boil. 'Swearing like a wich-waller' was proverbial. Special tools known as 'loots' were used like a hoe to pull salt to the side of the pan.

In 1527 complaints were made that 'foreigners' from Hartford and Le Cross were making salt. Old men testified that only men (*sic*) from Witton were allowed to make salt. Boiling was strictly limited to the period between Palm Sunday and Christmas. Transport was difficult in the winter and moving heavy loads would destroy road surfaces. It also helped to maintain prices by limiting production.

Officials were appointed annually. The Leadlookers supervised the process and times of boiling, recording the details in the 'Walling Book'. Pan Cutters removed a small piece so that they could not be overfilled. The Salt Viewers inspected quality while Killers of Salt were responsible for buying and selling salt and maintaining prices. The profits of two days and nights' boiling, called the 'peecing', were distributed among the poor.

Witton cum Twambrooks still belonged to the Barons of Kinderton. The Leftwich family owned that manor until it passed by marriage to the Oldfields in the 17th century. Ralph Leftwich left for Virginia in 1658, buying land in Kent County. In 1992 a party of descendants set up a monument on the site of Leftwich Hall. Later Wincham Hall was held by the Lee family, ancestors of General Robert E. Lee of the Confederate Army. Stones Manor Lane in Hartford was named after a misunderstanding; the founder of Hartford, Connecticut in fact came from Hertford, Herts.

The last of the Winningtons died in 1506 and his 14-year-old daughter Elizabeth was married to Peter Warburton of Arley to consolidate their estates. Lady Mary, the heiress of Holford Hall, Plumley, married Thomas, younger son of the Cholmondeleys, establishing a new branch of that family. She purchased Vale Royal from the Holcrofts, who had created a grand house out of the Abbey's domestic buildings. She entertained James I there in 1615. Extensive rebuilding took place at Vale Royal, Winnington, Leftwich, Arley, Wincham and other Halls. The Lordship of Rudheath extended from Witton to Holmes Chapel. The open common land had been a sanctuary 'for poor offenders who had casually fallen into criminal acts'. This local version of Sherwood Forest originated as a place where someone accused of crime might go to escape violence for guidance or to do penance. It degenerated into a haunt of 'wilful and desperate transgressors'. It lost its sanctuary status with the Reformation but its reputation for lawless inhabitants was to last for centuries. An early spelling is Reeds-heath, but this became corrupted along with its reputation, for 'ruddy' means bloodstained.

A new stone bridge was built with two arches in 1662. Above the central support was a projection where people could stand while heavy salt wagons passed. These were pulled by up to eight horses or oxen. Later footpaths overhanging the river were added.

In 1656 Daniel King wrote: 'And now, where this wedding is kept between Weaver and Dane the one as the Groom embracing the other in his bosome as his Bride, and uniting them and uniting both names into that one of Weaver, we see Northwich, the third of those salt making wiches so renowned for that commodity, a very ancient towen as the buildings and situation may well testifie. The chief Lordship whereof appertans to the right Honourable the Earl of Derby. A market town well frequented, gives its name to the hundred and seated so near the midst of the County, and so well for travel every way that it seems fit and is oft allotted to the meetings of the chief Governors in the County, for their great affairs. One street thereof called Wytton, yeild obedience to the Fee and Barony of Kinderton, the chief owner of them, and the whole Town, within the chapelry, for so they term'it, though it have a very fair Church called Wytton, the name of that Lordship mounted aloft upon a bank, that overviews the town of Northwich and is their Church, though a member, as I take it of Great Budworth Parish.'

In 1602 King James left Scotland to become King of England; during his sea journey a storm broke out which he was convinced was the work of witches. Throughout his reign persecution of witches reached fever pitch. Thomas Harrison, called 'the Northwich Deamonic' (possessed of deamons) was said to be cursed by local witches the same year. The symptoms, described by a Mr Harvey, were continual wagging of the head, supernatural strength, senselessness during fits and uttering sounds 'as are impossible to proceed from any human creature'. It might have been cerebral palsy.

Bishop Vaughan of Chester was more enlightened, instructing that he was to be kept away from crowds gathering to stare at him. He forbade any form of exorcism but specified seven ministers who were to stay with him, praying and reading from the Bible. It might have been a coincidence, but 'seven parsons' were believed to have great power against the occult. The case attracted much interest and formed the basis of a book on witchcraft published in London in 1617.

Other problems occupied people before that year ended. Plague started to the west of the town. A lodger there visited plague-stricken Nantwich and she carried it home. The registers at Witton Church record 250 deaths from plague including 'Humphrey Phitheon, clerk, curate of Witton, an honourable man'.

The problem must have been made worse by lack of water, for the main well was in Tabley Street called 'Down T'Well'. Water from the Dane, already polluted by other villages, was the only supply for laundry.

Arley Hall (reconstruction) with gatehouse and reception rooms in the front and a great hall across the courtyard. (AE)

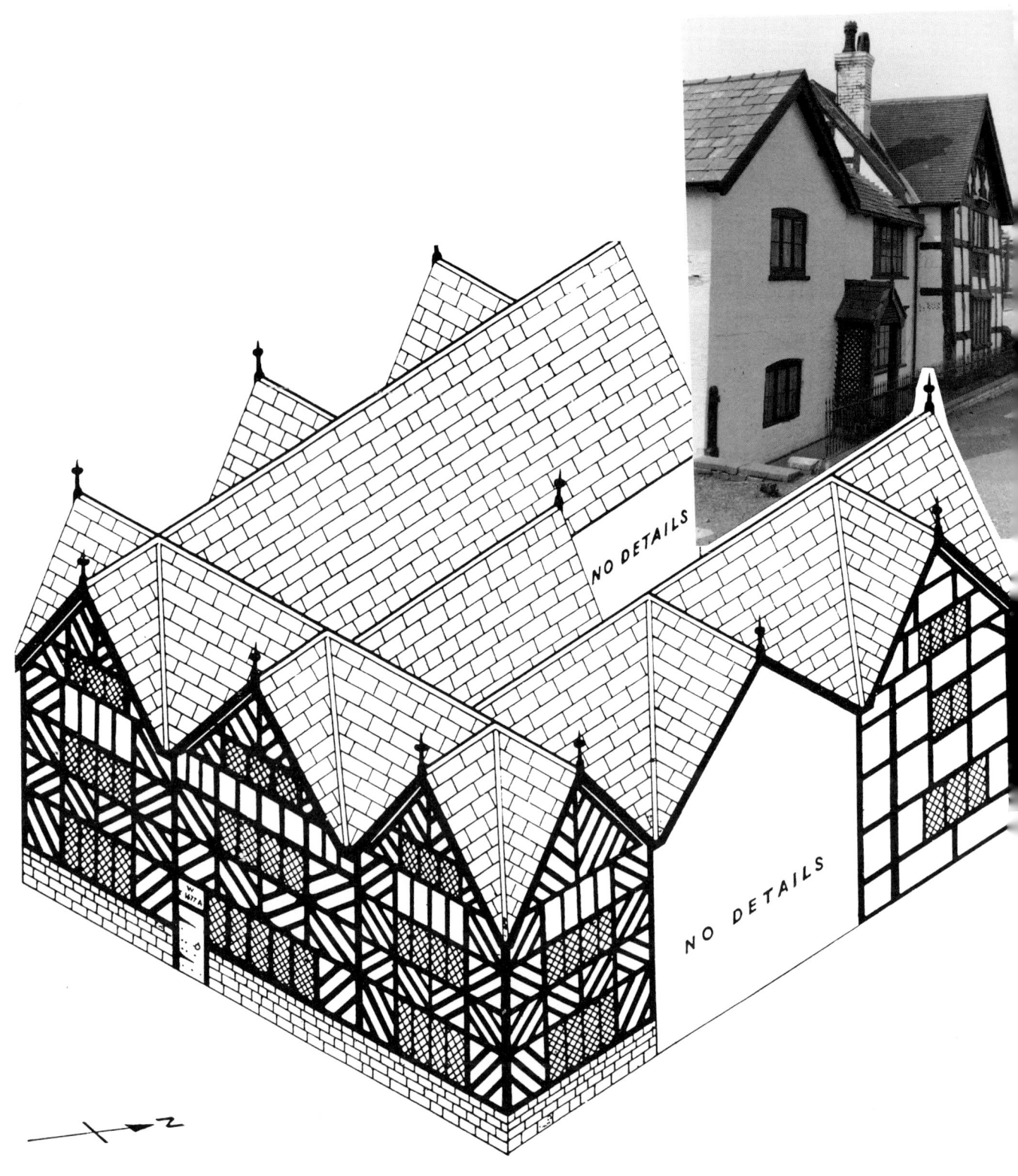

Undecorated timbering at Winnington Hall, probably 17th century. (ICI) INSET: Works House, (Platt's Hall) Lostock; the timber is dated 1665. (NC)

Parliamentarian Stronghold

Puritan clergy were active locally before the Civil War. From 1640-43 John Ley, 'Pastor of Great Budworth' published eight pamphlets criticising Archbishop Laud's reforms. In 1645 his pamphlet defending Cromwell's Parliament described him as 'a famous puritan Divine'. In 1648 he presided at a meeting of 59 ministers in Northwich agreeing Puritan worship. Under Cromwell he became Chairman of Parliament's Committee for Examining and Ordaining Ministers and its Committee for Printing. Numerous theological publications flowed from his pen, some written with Archbishop Usher, who calculated the date of Creation from Bible evidence as 4004 BC.

Ley's successor, James Livesay, refused to sign the 1662 Act of Uniformity (of worship). As a Dissenter he was 'ejected' from the church. Peter Earle, the Curate of Witton, left the same year. Also ejected was Adam Martindale, Vicar of neighbouring Rostherne, whose diaries record much information about the period. He was offered Witton Chapel in 1640 but accepted Rostherne as Witton provided less money and influence. His son was appointed Master at Witton Grammar School in 1679, attracting many new pupils, but in 1680 a 'deadly fever raged in the town' and the master fell victim. Livesay performed the funeral service as the victim was his son-in-law.

Ejected ministers continued conducting Nonconformist worship in houses and open places. Martindale records that a Northwich official issued a precept forbidding religious meetings outside Anglican churches. Believing this was beyond the law he came to Northwich for trial but was pursuaded to leave by Peter Earle, the Minister of Witton, who smoothed the matter over, despite personal risk.

Mid-Cheshire could not escape the devastating effects of the Civil War. Initially Cheshire was Royalist but, following the defeat of Royalist forces at Nantwich on 25 January 1643, Northwich became a Parliamentarian stronghold.

The Royalists under Sir Thomas Aston fled to Middlewich where they positioned their cannons in the churchyard. Captain Spotswood and a group of Royalist dragoons took control of Northwich, but were forced to retreat by Sir William Brereton, who garrisoned Northwich for Parliament.

From there on 13 March 1643, he attacked Middlewich at dawn. At the same time the foot regiments marched from Nantwich. The Royalists tried to re-position the cannon, causing alarm among their own men, who did not trust their aim. Many crammed into the church 'wedged up like billets in a wood-pile, no man at his arms'. Major Lothian, of the Nantwich foot, shot the door open and those inside surrendered.

Brereton was appointed Commander-in-Chief of Parliamentarian forces in Cheshire, constructing a fortification overlooking Town Bridge by Winnington Hill. He suppressed all local opposition from there. Dr William Bentley, a 17th century dissenter, used the earthworks as a garden, and was buried in a summer house on its summit in 1680. All traces were destroyed by subsidence.

On 18 August 1644 Colonel John Marrow headed a Royalist cavalry regiment from Chester to take Northwich. The garrison met them at Hartford. Before retreating they took 15 Northwich men prisoner. Marrow was 'shott in Sandiwaye by one lying under a hedge' and died the following day in Chester.

Prince Rupert, the Royalist hero, was expected to attack Northwich on his journey through Cheshire and Lancashire to the decisive Battle of Marston Moor. Katharine Stubbs appealed for compensation in 1650 as the garrison 'caused ffawer bays of her building to be pulled down for feare of giveing advantage to the enimyes'.

Tradition says that Cromwell shot a cross from the tower of Witton Church, putting his foot on a fragment of a (Roman?) column which survives on Highfield Hill. Cromwell never came to Northwich.

The registers of Witton Church state that no entries were recorded at that time because of the 'Flying [fleeing] of clerks'. Marks on the south of the tower are said to be caused by musket balls. Their position suggests they may have been caused by a firing squad.

Parliamentarian troops under General Lambert attacked Vale Royal in 1644, burning the south wing. It was claimed that the only things left behind were silver plate hidden in a secret drawer and the children's pony, hidden behind panelling!

The final battle between Royalist and Roundhead took place in 1659 at Winnington Bridge. George Booth raised the rebellion. His intention was not primarily to restore the Monarchy. He sat in the Long Parliament, fought for Parliament in the Civil War and served in Cromwell's Parliament. Like others he became dissatisfied and disillusioned after the death of Oliver Cromwell the year previously, as Cromwell's son was easily manipulated by the army.

Booth, with other Cheshire gentlemen, intended to take Chester and march on London. They could not occupy Chester for, although the Mayor had Royalist sympathies, the Castle was held by a strong force of Parliamentarians who smuggled out a request for reinforcements. Booth's forces withdrew to Northwich, where they spent the night of 18 August. General Lambert, with professional forces of Cromwell's New Model Army, marched from Nantwich, camping at Weaverham. Booth's forces crossed Town Bridge on the morning of 19 August and met Lambert's at Hartford Beach.

The rebels were forced back to the river at Winnington. Pressed by the pursuing Model Army they crowded onto the narrow bridge. Gentlemen on horseback and untrained men on foot tried to force their way over to regroup and defend the crossing. It was hopeless! Some were forced into the river and others tried to escape by scrambling up the banks to Barnton. Lambert allowed those on foot to make their way home but pursued the horsemen to Frodsham, Warrington and Manchester. The Royalists lost thirty men, Lambert just one.

A week later an inn keeper in Buckinghamshire became suspicious of 'Mistress Dorothy', who arrived without any women in her retinue. She was tall, with large shoes and a manly walk. He notified the authorities when the men tried to buy the barber's razor. The 'Mistress' was George Booth, who was sent to the Tower but was released a few months later. The following year Parliament invited Charles II to return.

The decision to head for Northwich could have been influenced by Brereton's defences. Lord Derby and Thomas Cholmondeley of Vale Royal, in Booth's band with local contacts, would have made them expect help and shelter. Derby was arrested after the rebellion, dressed as a serving man. His father was a leading Royalist who held the Isle of Man and mounted a revolt from there. He was defeated at Wigan, sentenced at Chester and beheaded at Bolton in 1651.

Sometimes the battle is wrongly described as the last battle of the Civil War. It was, however, the last time Roundhead and Royalist met in battle.

A significant contribution to the Royalist cause was made by Sir John Birkenhead. Born in Witton Chapelry in 1615, and a pupil of Witton Grammar School he gained an MA at Oxford, becoming secretary to Archbishop Laud. The King set up court at Oxford in January 1643, where Laud introduced Birkenhead, securing his appointment as editor of a newspaper called *Mercurius Aulicus*. It was published without fail every week up to the fall of the Royalist cause in Autumn 1650.

It was the first newspaper of modern style with editorial comments, a leader column and accurate reporting. Birkenhead is recognised as 'the father of English journalism'. When the Royalists were defeated, Birkenhead fled the country. In 1660, he was elected to the Restoration Parliament and knighted for his services in the war, becoming a founder-member of the Royal Society.

Following the exile of Charles II Continental craftsmen and artisans were encouraged to come to this country. They may have introduced the first salt pans, made from iron sheets, allowing larger pans to be made. As a result the old formal method of salt making declined. Northwich changed from a small market town with a part-time salt industry to a thriving industrial town.

The changes did not come without misfortune to some. The Grammar School lost a reliable part of its income; nothing was earned from the founder's salt house after 1677. Others fared worse. Ralph Broome sank his own salt well which failed, making him bankrupt; in 1713 he fled the town. Ralph and Thomas Nickson's business failed and the latter left for 'one of the plantacions in America'. Fortunes were made and lost by many in Northwich in the following centuries.

In 1642 Dr William Bentley purchased this house. In 1643 Brereton built fortifications behind.

LEFT: Sir William Brereton. (AM) RIGHT: George Booth, whose rebellion was crushed. (AM) BELOW: Winnington Bridge.

Beacon of the Industrial Revolution

The Industrial Revolution saw the change in production from cottage industries with people working at home to the factory system. The origins of these revolutionary changes are associated with the Darby family, ironfounders of Coalbrookdale, and Arkwright's conversion of spinning to factory production. The development of canals by the Duke of Bridgewater and the harnessing of steam power by James Watt provided the other major changes. All four founding fathers had associations with the district.

In effect, the Northwich salt industry passed through these changes before other areas. The conversion of salt manufacture from wood to coal occurred following the Restoration, when the use of iron pans was introduced. Limits on using wood as fuel (introduced after the Spanish Armada to preserve wood for ship-building) must have had an influence.

There was no contemporary account of the change and the term 'leads' was used for pans even through they were made of iron. In 1585, 453 pans were recorded but only 23 were working in 1682. There was no reduction in the demand for salt but fewer and larger iron pans were used. They were some of the largest iron objects at the time and fore-runners of the Industrial Revolution's use of iron.

Contemporary accounts mention several brine-pits, indicating that the old ordered system had collapsed. The salt industry had passed from the 'domestic' stage, with small-scale work under strict limits supervised by a sort of guild, into full-scale industrial practice. Salt works of the 17th century employed men and women to work in factory conditions a century before Arkwright's mills. The work changed from part time-employment to a full-time job. However, it was not until the present century that the process was mechanised.

Prospecting for coal locally proved futile but in 1670 William Marbury at Marbury discovered a bed of rock salt with a stream of brine running along the surface.

In 1698, Celia Fiennes passed through Northwich writing. 'Its not very large, its full of Salt works the brine pitts being all here and about and so they make all things convenient to follow the makeing of salt, so that the town is full of smoak from the salterns on all sides; they have within these few yeares found in their brine pitts a hard Rocky salt that lookes cleer like sugar candy, and its taste shews it to be Salt, they call this Rock salt; it will make very good brine with fresh water to use quickly, this they carry to the water side into Wales and by those rivers that are flow'd with the tyde's in, which produces a strong and good salt as the others; there were 12 salterns together at Northwich'.

Salt works at Frodsham and Liverpool had been established by 1700 where rock salt was mixed with tidal sea water. It was easier to export form there and saved the cost of carrying coal to Northwich. Rock salt was also mixed with weak brine to improve production locally. It was fashionable for intellectuals to visit salt works or mines as coaching routes passed through Northwich. Daniel Defoe was one in 1724 but he found them 'not so very strange that we came away not extremely gratified in our curiosity'.

In 1658 William Webb wrote of the Weaver that it had 'of late swelled and foamed too impatiently because it may not be employed with boats and carriages from the Mersey mouth, which it thinks itself sufficient enough for, if it was cleared of some weres and stoppages'. From 1721 this was effected and Northwich grew to prominence in the salt industry. The navigation of the river made it possible to import coal easily and export the salt in the same barges which arrived black and left white.

One development related to salt works was one of the earliest iron-smelting furnaces of the Industrial Revolution at Vale Royal, working between 1690 and 1790. The site cannot now be identified — the term Royal Vale was used for the whole Weaver valley. A furnace close to the mansion is unlikely and it would need to be at a point where the river bank is steep. Furnaces were built into banks where the fuel and ore were continually loaded at the top while the molten iron ran into the moulds at the bottom. Romans had smelted iron on Castle, the monks has a 'bloomery' (smelting furnace) and the furnace may have improved an existing industry, perhaps near Hartford Bridge.

In 1716 the furnace was taken over by Abraham Darby of Coalbrookdale, who seven years before made the first cast-iron, using coke. It was one of the largest in the country then, smelting ore from Cumbria, with coal from Lancashire. As it was not near these sources its position is explained by the demand for sheets of iron for salt pans. Loose coal and ore were easier to move on horseback than metal sheets. The Navigation transported coal while ore could be delivered the same way. This made a viable proposition which probably attracted Darby's interest.

The operation of salt mines improved after 1788 when John Gilbert installed a steam engine produced by the Birmingham partnership of James Watt and Matthew Boulton. This was installed only two years after they sold their first engine. Developed for pumping water from coal and tin mines, later steam engines delivered a continual supply of brine to the pans.

The progress of the Marshall family who became the foremost producers of salt during the 18th century demonstrates the development of the industry. The family originated in Nantwich as shoemakers and owned a wich house.

In 1720 Thomas Marshall moved to Northwich, arriving the year before the Weaver Navigation Act. A survey of 1733 recorded 17 salt pans, nine of them owned by the Barrow family. Others were still owned by local gentry and there were nine rock salt mines. Around 1734 Marshall took a lease on Baron's Croft (where the courts are now) and built pan-sheds, a brine reservoir and a cistern for refining rock salt. The demand for salt was so great that an extra brine supply *via* hollowed elm logs was provided. His business expanded, leasing works at Anderton and Winnington. He purchased Witton Hey Wood for a salt mine, which collapsed because of 'unscientific' mining.

His house, Brineseath Brow, on Winnington Hill, survives with the Counting (accounting) House from which the salt empire was controlled, on the other side of the road. A former stable makes up Marshall's Place.

Marshall's success was possible because he had capital to invest and established links with Liverpool merchants using his own fleet of flats to bring good coal from St Helen's to his own wharves on the Dane and Witton Brook. He had access to fine brine and rock salt on his own land.

The first Thomas Marshall died in 1772 and was succeeded by his son, Thomas. In 1779 a lower, richer bed of rock salt was discovered at Lawton. Marshall was the first to mine this bed in Northwich from a mine called Dunkirk, after the port used for exports. Visitors could explore the 'immense solemn and awful temple' 300 feet below ground. In 1796 a Boulton and Watt steam winding engine was installed there.

He was keen to improve transport for salt and raw materials. He purchased the Lordship of the manor of Drakelow cum Rudheath in 1776, the year that the Trent and Mersey Canal was dug through it, establishing the busy little wharf at Broken Cross. He was instrumental in gaining the connection between the river and the canal at Anderton. In attempts to fix salt prices he formed associations with other salt manufacturers.

Diversifying investments, he had interests in one of the earliest cotton mills built beside the Weaver (for delivery of cotton bales) by his brother-in-law, Mr Page, started in 1780 when the patent for water-frames was held by Arkwright under licence from him. It was completed in 1784 a year before the patent was lost. Arkwright must have authorised the mill and may have advised on its design. Stones on the bank of the Dane near the Memorial Hall are from the weir which was constructed by Marshall upstream of his wharfs to create a head of water. It redirected water by way of a canal and tunnel (The Cut) constructed by Marshall over his land. Water fell onto a water wheel in the mill, turning leather belts which powered the water-frames.

Hand-loom cotton weaving was established before 1775 when Marshall built New Street on part of Baron's Croft. It was lined by three-storey brick houses with 'weavers' lofts' on the top floor. Spinning was undertaken by women in mills while men did weaving in the home. The mill with near-by weavers' cottages is reminiscent of Cromford. When the mill was destroyed by fire in 1799, Marshall used the wheel to pump brine. The site on Baron's Quay is now Moore and Brock's builders merchants.

The second Marshall purchased Hartford Greenbank Manor House in 1774, adding fashionable reception rooms, and establishing the family among the land-owners of Mid-Cheshire.

An important comtemporary (1739-1808) was Richard Pennant, Lord Penrhyn, who added the elegant Regency wing to Winnington Hall in 1773, probably designed by Samuel Wyatt. He married Anne Susannah, heiress of General Hugh Warburton of Winnington. They each owned half of Penrhyn's rich slate quarries. Warburton established the traditional names used for slate sizes. Penrhyn's family owned sugar plantations in Jamaica and he made a fortune from the slave trade.

The Winnington Estates were used for salt making and salt was a vital part of the 'triangular trade'. It was sent with other products *via* Liverpool to West Africa to be bartered for slaves. They were loaded into the same ships which followed the trade winds to the West Indies. There slaves were replaced by sugar or cotton for the return journey, following the Gulf Stream. Much of Northwich's prosperity was built on salt and the slave trade, and slave traders used their profits to buy homes such as Bostock Hall and Hefferston Grange.

While the cotton mill was being built, Penrhyn asked his agent to see if any of his lands were suited for cotton growing. Penrhyn was one of Liverpool's MPs and spoke often in the Commons, defending and promoting the slave trade, becoming known as the 'Member for the West Indies'.

He was a pioneer of the Industrial Revolution, improving trade for his vast slate quarries at Penrhyn so that slate became the universal roofing material. He developed the North Wales coast road and built the Avenue at Winnington as a drive to the Hall, along which his funeral procession took his body to Llandygai Church in 1808.

The same year pictures of Winnington Hall and Bridge went to Russia on the dinner service made for Catherine the Great by Wedgewood. They were painted by Samuel Stringer, one of a family of Knutsford painters. His father painted the original Blue Cap and Smoker pub signs and his brother Daniel trained at the Royal Academy but took to drink and died at Northwich.

Between 1693 and 1825 salt was taxed; it was fixed at two shillings a bushel in 1696 and paid when salt left the works. This limited opening of salt works to those with sufficient capital to pay the tax and recoup the money when it was sold. Many stories survive, telling how people outwitted the Revenue Men (tax collectors), supplying farmers with salt for bacon, dairy and domestic use. Rudheath was the centre for salt smugglers called 'freebooters'. Romper Lowe, a gang leader, would sit in inns with bags as if ready for smuggling. The Revenue men waited to catch him in the act while his gang were busily hiding salt in Rudheath Woods.

A Shipbrook tale is of a skeleton coated with phosphorus glowing in the dark to scare people away from the smugglers. Many tricks were used to outwit the Revenue Men and smuggling was something of a sport. A Revenue Man, suspicious of the number of funerals crossing Rudheath, forced a coffin open, finding it full of salt. Women took food into the works and left with bags of salt suspended under their skirts, where Revenue Men could not search. Northwich had more tax collectors than any other town in the country and smuggling was an accepted way of life.

During this time of change, the ownership of the manors passed to entrepreneurs who changed the town more than in all the centuries before. Lord Derby sold the manor of Northwich with the revenues from markets and fairs to John Mort, a leading salt proprietor, by Act of Parliament in 1784. Mort encouraged the building of the cotton mill and built the Yorkshire Buildings in 1786, where fairs were held lasting for two weeks. Goods from Manchester and Yorkshire were a speciality, hence the name. Mort's son Jonadab died in 1799, willing Northwich to his sister, who married Thomas Wakefield. They became bankrupt in 1803 as they could not pay salt duties. Arthur Heywood, a Liverpool banker, purchased the manorial rights. In 1870 the Local Board purchased them from John Heywood.

The Countess of Abingdon, last of the Venables, died in 1715. The title Baron of Kinderton and Witton Manor passed to the Vernons of Sudbury, Derbyshire. In 1745 they sold Witton to Sir Peter Leicester of Tabley. It was sold as separate lots from 1826 to '29. A map surveyed for the sale, along with descriptions of each lot, forms one of the most accurately detailed descriptions of any town at that date. The sale allowed development without permission from the manorial lord, and investors purchased property to speculate.

Castle was part of the estate of John Tollemache of Peckforton Castle, who developed workers' housing as an investment. After the death of Lord Penrhyn, Winnington was sold to Lord Stanley of Alderley. He was a descendent of Thomas Stanley, who was granted Northwich in 1484 and was made guardian of the heiress of Weaver (south of Winsford) by Henry VII. He married her to his second son, founding this branch of the family. Edward John Stanley occupied the Hall from 1842 to '52. His involvement as an MP in five Governments meant that his wife and children were left there and virtually ignored. She exchanged numerous letters with her mother-in-law which were published by Nancy Mitford.

She had been a noted beauty, but the letters reveal that after 33 years of, presumably, happy marriage she seems to have been dumped in the country and he did not even visit them at Christmas. His duties in the House can only partly explain his attitude. She complained about the shabby house and draughts to her mother-in-law, and in 1850 when they succeeded to Alderley she left Winnington. The pretence of a happy Victorian marriage was kept up and she is shown in a brass portrait on his tomb at Alderley as a loving mother with four grown-up sons, five daughters, two infants and a baby. He is shown in a separate effigy.

18th century wall painting of Marbury Hall (Hall Farm, Acton Bridge), shows boating, hare coursing and a negro servant (slave?) on horseback behind the carriage. (NC) RIGHT: Lord Penrhyn MP, slave trader and pioneer of change. (NT) CENTRE: The Girls of Miss Bell's Academy promenade outside the arched windows of Penrhyn's Winnington Hall orangery. (ICI) BELOW: Penrhyn's hen house had perches for 600 birds and food preparation rooms. (ICI)

ABOVE: The 'Ass-ociation' cartoon (1834) mocked associations formed to fix salt prices. (CM) BELOW: Typical of engines produced after Boulton and Watt's patent ended, this one was installed at Littler's Mine, Marston in 1810, going to the Science Museum in 1910. (NC)

A Smoking Hell-hole

When Ruskin visited Winnington Hall he avoided Northwich, calling it 'a smoking Hell hole'.

The Victorian town was a warren of narrow streets erected without planning or any restrictions. Control of any sort over Witton ended when it was sold in individual lots from 1827-9, allowing anyone to build as they wanted. It was only after the creation of the Urban District Council in 1894 that this free-for-all came under control.

The good example of New Street and Yorkshire Buildings was followed by poor quality developments. Houses were interspersed with salt works and workshops. Though houses were built as reasonable dwellings, lack of regulation often saw them degenerate into shabby lodging houses.

There was always demand for beds as people came from Ireland and country areas, because of constant demand for unskilled labour in salt or chemical works. They intended spending a short time here, working as part of the emigration process. Hard work in terrible conditions accumulated the price of a ticket from Liverpool to a new life. This sometimes started by working a passage to Liverpool.

Sanitation hardly existed, washing facilities were basic, while pigs, poultry and other livestock lived around, and often in dwellings. In 1832 cholera arrived from Asia, spreading quickly in the tightly packed filthy slums. The entrance to Crown Street was roped off. A notice forbade entry and an isolation hospital opened in Timber Lane. No-one knew the cause or cure but a provident dispensary, where people paid weekly for medicines, stayed open despite the risk to the proprietor. A passing Methodist minister was persuaded to preach in Leftwich Chapel, saying he felt the worst was over. Then the epidemic eased, resulting in many converts.

In 1837 the workhouse was built for those who could not pay their way. Families were separated on entry and married couples or parents and children rarely met. Men, women, boys and girls each had their own quadrangle of wards enclosing four 'airing yards'. Each group walked around separately for exercise and to freshen the uniforms they had to wear. Jobless from as far away as Winsford and Middlewich were sent there, while conditions were unpleasant to deter those unwilling to work.

Inmates had to work for their living and it was designed like a factory with a clock to regulate work. One room was for 'picking oakum' *ie:* pulling old ropes apart with finger-nails, to be used in boat building for water-tight packing between planks. A laundry was operated and the charges reduced running costs.

Food was basic. Canon France-Hayhurst of Bostock provided special meals for the 1897 Jubilee. Two eggs, bread and butter with coffee was breakfast, dinner was cold meat with salad, pickles, bread and butter followed by a fruit pie and a pint of beer to drink the Queen's health. Tea was cake with bread and butter. This, they were told, 'should have made it the happiest day they had ever experienced'!

There was an isolation ward for anyone with infectious diseases from the town, and cells where the Governor put offenders in solitary confinement without trial. Unmarried mothers-to-be were sent in disgrace to give birth there. Children attended the workhouse school to prevent opportunity of escape. It became an old persons' home and in 1968 had residents who were born there as illegitimate children and had never left.

A separate structure provided overnight accommodation for vagrants. The large 1891 extension contained a room where people applied for 'outdoor relief'. Surrounded by grim portraits of local worthies they faced a panel of equally grim 'Guardians' to explain why they could not find work. They had to sell everything but bare essentials to raise money before receiving a penny.

A lock-up was built when the 1832 Reform Bill outlawed the stocks. It was hardly better as it was affected by subsidence and the cells had several inches of water on the floor. Water flowed in the County Court when the rivers flooded. J. H. Cooke recalled standing on chairs to address the Judge, who would not adjourn. Lawyers were carried out of court on workmen's backs while Judge Harden left by carriage.

The lock-up was used for drunks to sleep off the effects overnight and there was ample opportunity to get drunk. Fourteen beer-houses and thirty-four hotels, inns or taverns were licensed in 1860. Some were only one room in a cottage. The Crown Hotel was the leading establishment where auction sales were held, including the sale of the Manor of Witton. It was a Posting and Commercial House, indicating that stage coaches stopped there to change horses and collect or deliver mail. It had accommodation for commercial travellers. They carried samples from large stores or manufacturers and hired a sitting room where respectable customers visited to see samples and place orders. A horse drawn omnibus met trains at Hartford Station four times a day.

In the Crown and Anchor farmers and merchants got together with samples of grain to agree prices. Men were hired, trade agreements were made and property was exchanged in public houses, confirmed by a handshake.

The Lion and Railway, Greenbank and Railway at Hartford had sitting rooms which families could hire to wait for trains. They had large stables to leave horses or a horse and carriage could be hired to complete the journey. A painted advert for Nancollis' Temperance Hotel (where no alcohol was allowed) survives near the Station.

'Pop Hornby', botanical brewer, served non-alcoholic cordials. The original brewer was a lock-keeper at Hunts Lock, gathering local herbs. His son opened a shop in Witton Street in 1895, decorated with etchings showing a family ruined by alcohol.

A Local Board was formed, adopting the Local Government Act of 1863 which empowered them to levy rates to provide schools and other services. Its authority was extended in 1880 to include Northwich, Witton, and parts of Hartford, Winnington and Leftwich. On 10 September 1894 this was constituted as a civil parish under the name of Northwich, with an Urban District Council responsible for 1,285 acres of dry land and 112 of water.

The Local Board purchased the market rights from the Heywood family and improved the facilities. A market hall was erected in 1875; beams from it inscribed 'Manor of Northwich' are preserved in Vicarsway Park. Stalls could be removed and it was used for large assemblies. In 1887 geese caused problems as hundreds were walked to market. John McArdle was fined 10s for refusing to move more than 600 birds which blocked the street. The same court sentenced two men to a month in prison for stealing six pennyworth of potatoes from a field in Witton.

Provision of public services was affected by subsidence. Early in the century water was provided from a reservoir at Winnington. In 1857 a limited company opened Northwich Waterworks at Wade Brook. Water was raised by vertical wheel into a tank 120 feet above

High Street, delivering 40,000 gallons daily. Points were provided on the mains for fighting fires, without charge, the pressure sufficient for the highest buildings. Its purity was suspect and the Mayor of Over caused embarrassment, commenting on muddy drinking water served when the Library was opened.

The Northwich Gas Company provided gas for lighting. A by-product was coke, sold for domestic fires and carried home in barrows or buckets. A respected cure for coughs, colds or whooping cough was inhaling Gas Works fumes. Salt miners were free of such illnesses. When people were ill sawdust was scattered outside to quieten iron cart-wheels and clogs.

Poor children went with a bucket and poker to search salt works tips for cinders and bits of coal for the one domestic fire providing heat for cooking and warming water. Without them and scavenged wood the house remained cold.

Many industries were linked to salt production. An Elizabethan monopoly was held by the Gorst family for making conical baskets called 'barrows' or 'peg tops'. A normal one and a miniature (used to send fine salt to London) were made in 1893 for the Salt Museum by the last maker. Barrows, or peg tops were made by splitting a hazel branch several times length-wise, leaving a short piece uncut at the end. Wood-shavings (not wicker) were woven between the segments to form a cone. Wet salt was poured in, to set as a block. Later they were replaced by elmwood tubs giving a voissoir shape, ideal for building the salt arches set up for Victorian celebrations.

Timber yards provided for the salt and other trades. Logs were delivered by boat to Baron's Quay and taken to Littler's Yard on timber limbers. These were separate front and rear wheel bogies attached to logs of any length. Shire horses pulled them from wharves in Leicester Street. When traffic was clear in Witton Street the horses rushed up the bank and over into Ship Hill, now the entrance to the Shopping Centre.

Wood was split into planks by circular saw, machines planed it smooth or reproduced carvings on planks which were used to decorate shop-fronts. Planed or decorated wood distinguishes Northwich buildings from adze-cut Tudor ones. A branch linked Baron's Quay to the Station for delivery of heavy building materials.

Furniture makers produced items from chairs and tables to dolly-pegs and rolling-pins. The Leicester family of Plumley stamped chairs with their name, which were taken all over the country. Some are in a museum in Leicester as they were believed to have been made there.

The demand for iron goods was enormous and in 1860 two foundries (Bates' and Gibson's) operated. When Bates' foundry closed equipment was taken to the Ironbridge Museum, reforging an historic link. They made iron pipes for saltpans and numerous domestic items. Drain covers locally still carry the Bates name.

Joseph Parks specialised in structural steel-work, making joists for reinforced buildings which replaced timber frames for 'liftable' buildings. Unfounded local tradition says they made Sydney Harbour Bridge.

Boat-yards (seven in 1860) contained foundries and forges besides carpenters and paint-shops. The vessels were launched into the river sideways as they were longer than it was wide. Coastal vessels and river-boats were built.

A modern boat repair shed with sideways launching ramps survives by Northwich Pond (the area between the bridges) and a dock by Hayhurst Bridge. The Weaver Navigation yards produced numerous items for the Navigation up to the size of lock-gates. Many narrow-boats have 'Northwich' painted on them, showing they are registered here. Canal boats were decorated with the traditional castles and roses and a workshop at Anderton provided decorated water-cans and buckets.

The Weaver Navigation Buildings date from 1829. The main block was for the Trustees, with a handsome fan-light over the door. The Donkey Field opposite was kept for grazing so that the Trustees were not overlooked. A second block, to the side, was set back with a separate entrance for senior clerks. An iron fence prevents use of the corner as a urinal. Near to the river were offices for the junior clerks and a shelter where boatmen waited to pay dues.

In 1860 there were four marine store dealers, three in Church Street, who were rag and bone merchants giving day-old chicks in exchange. Bones were roasted and then ground in tanks of water by huge stones pushed by power from steam engines in mills, including Wincham Wharf and a bone and glue works at Leftwich. Bone-meal was used as fertilizer and is the main component of bone china.

Cheshire's dairy industry provided bones, and hides for Dutton's leather works in Queen Street, who used local salt and barks for tanning. Also in Leftwich, Henry Holland was a fellmonger dealing in skins and hides.

Up to the Second World War wooden-soled clogs with iron protectors and leather uppers were worn by most workers. In salt works they protected feet from splashes of brine. Rags tied around the ankles for protection were called 'buskins' (Latin for sandals). Each clog was shaped to fit around the wearer's bunions. Wooden blocks (usually alder) were cut to shape by long-handled knives hooked into the bench at one end with a lever action of the left hand, moving the block around with his right.

There were several rope-walks, including part of Navigation Road and one to the north of the Drill Field. The rope maker walked backwards, adding fibres while twisting with a special tool called a 'twistrel'. It was a metal hook passed through a tubular handle and bent in two opposing right angles.

Off Station Road was Yates Court, or 'Clay Pipe Alley', where tobacco pipes were made and sold at a penny a dozen, for pubs to give away with tobacco. Cornish clay came *via* the Weaver. It was founded in 1832 by William Yates and his sister. Her son continued the business until it was destroyed by fire in 1913. Other trades included coach-makers, wheelwrights, blacksmiths, nail-makers, braziers and tin-smiths. There were builders and builders' merchants, stone-masons and ironmongers. Women operated businesses as straw bonnet makers, milliners and dress-makers (15 in 1860). Before the invention of the sewing machine clothing was hand sewn and many married women were paid for sewing or laundry at home between house-work. Men ran linen and woollen drapers' shops; there were also hatters and an umbrella maker. Pawn-brokers carried on a flourishing trade, giving cash loans against household goods or clothes. Tea merchants had blending warehouses and three breweries employed coopers to make barrels. Brunner Mond had a cooperage for their products.

Farm-land came close to the town; in 1860 three farms existed in Witton Street. There was a cowkeeper, keeping milking cows in small enclosures for fresh deliveries. At harvest time and when potatoes were picked there was casual work irrespective of age or sex. Children were expected to earn their keep and were often missing from school when farmers were planting or harvesting. At Sandiway a school holiday was arranged for the first hunt so that children could work fetching and carrying. Canal boat children caused great concern to the NSPCC around 1890. They were left to operate locks or steer boats unsupervised despite risks. One father who had been reprimanded for cruelty to his sons sold them like slaves to work for another boatman.

Among obsolete manual jobs were tripe dressers, eel spearers, night-soil-men, lamp-lighters and knockers-up.

Northwich, surrounded by country estates belonging to titled gentry, wealthy industrialists and Liverpool merchants, always had employment for servants. Affording a servant was a middle class criterion. Larger houses in Hartford and Greenbank employed indoor servants, gardeners, coachman and stable hands. Houses in Church Road, built into the hill-side, had a half cellar for daily help to prepare food and to do laundry. Servants worked in public houses and hotels as maids, waitresses, cooks and ostlers. There were probably more people employed in service than in salt making. Entering service was preferred to factory work as it ensured a home and food. Good servants moved from lowly work to become housekeeper or butler managing a large staff.

ABOVE: Coombs' store, a prestige 1920s department store. (NC)
BELOW: The Dane Warehouse and gas-works yard c1880. In 1970 a first floor lintel showed above the water, but by 1990 it had sunk out of sight. (NC)

LEFT: Washing and mangling at a public wash-house: women 'took in' washing for a price. (CJL) RIGHT: Horse-drawn traffic, with obvious pollution, passed this shop. BELOW: This coaching inn (1762) has stables and cottages, built against existing walls. (TC)

LEFT: The Crown Hotel's cellar is 30ft below the present building. (NC)
RIGHT: Elam's was a land-mark in Witton Street. (NC) BELOW: When the first chip shop opened, the landlord here reputedly provided potatoes and a frying pan on the fire. (NC)

ABOVE: Eliza Leadbeater and barmaids at the Bull's Head, c1890. (CL)
BELOW: The old Cock Hotel, 1899. (NC)

ABOVE: The Waterman's Arms was one of many cottage-sized pubs. (CL) BELOW: The Penryhn Arms in New Street was where the police station was built. (CL)

ABOVE: This Congregational Chapel at the foot of Winnington Hill was used from 1853 to 1881. BELOW: The Waterman's Church on Castle Hill. (MH)

For Righteousness Sake

After the Civil War some still wanted to use simple forms of worship, following the teachings of the Swiss reformer Calvin. Because they dissented to sign the Act of Uniformity of 1662 they are known as Nonconformists or Dissenters.

Witton, a poor chapel, had difficulty attracting clergy. Curates were appointed by the Lord of the Manor after 1717. Some were social contacts chosen as a favour. They were university educated upper-class men, who entered the church for a respectable well-paid living, not out of missionary zeal, and had little sympathy for the poor. In the 18th century Witton was held by clergymen also responsible for other churches. The Curates of Great Budworth and Witton competed for fees to perform weddings and funerals. Witton did not become a separate parish until 7 August 1900, despite Hartford and Lostock becoming full parishes created from the chapelry. This explains an event of 1753. An elegantly dresed lady arrived at the Red Lion in Northwich, asking the landlord to produce a bridegroom — at once! He sent for a barber, who hesitated, so a linen draper's apprentice offered his services. They went to Budworth where the wedding could take place without the delay inevitable at Witton. As the register was signed two gentlemen with liveried servants arrived. She had an income of £800 a year which she intended to spend but her father had tried to marry her to a decrepit old miser.

A congregation of Dissenters was established at Lostock Green during the Civil War. The Conventicle Act, passed after the Restoration, forbade meetings of dissenters within five miles of any town. They had to demolish their chapel and move to Cape Farm on Holford Moss. The grave-yard was ploughed up and no trace survives.

It is not certain when the first Dissenting congregation was established in Northwich after the Act of Toleration (1689) removed restrictions. A minister was appointed in 1720 but left within two years. The first Dissenting chapel was built in Crown Street in 1748 but by 1759 the congregation had disbanded and the chapel was rented to Wesley's friend, Daniel Barker in 1762 for Methodists. Then the minister of Allostock started holding services there to keep them out and the dispute left the building locked up.

In 1795 Job Wilson, from Sowerby, was appointed Independent Minister, earning a reputation as a saint. At first he was shunned and people crossed the road to avoid him. Slowly he earned respect for hard work and good ways. His diary records during three months 'I preached seventy-five sermons and travelled about nine hundred miles, mostly on foot'.

He saw Crown Street Chapel rebuilt in 1806, then enlarged, and was buried there after dying in London on Queen Victoria's Coronation Day, 1837. His remains were moved to a chapel at the foot of Winnington Hill in 1853. When that was taken down because of subsidence they were moved again in 1880 to the Congregationalist chapel on Castle.

The indignity felt by Wilson was mild compared to the way early Methodists were treated. Northwich was one of the most hostile places in the land.

The Methodists tried to reach poor working men who were out of touch with the Anglican church. Word was put around rowdy people that Methodists were religious fanatics who would prevent them enjoying drink and other social pleasures. In the middle of the 18th century Methodists were liable to lose jobs or homes. By the end of the century they had earned a reputation for thrift, good living, sobriety and a basic education from Sunday School. Employers actively encouraged Methodists.

John Wesley regularly visited the district. The first time in May 1747 he preached at Mr Anderton's near Northwich, recording there were some rough persons present but also 'several of the gay and rich'.

Early preachers claimed they were thrown into The Cut and 'baptised' by angry mobs. Isaac Barnes, a seedsman and preacher, said he was 'often rolled in the foul cut'. The cotton mill cut was not completed until 1784, as least 20 years later. A weir and lock existed near Lock Street, until they were destroyed by the collapse of Metcalf's (Barons Quay) Mine when a temporary dam was set up. It is likely that the 'cut' was part of this. Moses Dale was carried around the town on a butcher's block as if for execution. In the Bull Ring the mob surrounded him, banging on cans and blowing cows' horns to mock hymn-singing until he was deafened. Converts had to be content with boycotting of their trade or were refused work. Several were forced to emigrate.

On Tuesday 3 August 1762 Wesley preached in the Crown Street Chapel, describing it as 'a little room that would hold about 40 people'. A mob gathered outside, becoming louder during the service. He was begged to stay in the Chapel until they dispersed but walked bravely through; mounting his horse, he rode to Manchester. Many things were thrown but none hit him. The following Friday he returned to preach in Mr Page's yard on Barons Quay. 'An abundance of people flocked together, nor did anyone oppose or make the least disturbance, and when I afterwards rode through the town, I had not one uncivil word'. In 1765 he passed through one Friday, returning to preach the next Monday morning and lunched at Gadbrook, a farmhouse where services were held.

On 7 April 1774 he preached when the foundation stone of a chapel was laid at Leftwich, (now Theatre Court). He wrote 'all persecution seems now to be at and end'. He preached at the opening service on 22 March 1775 and was back in 1779 and 1788. In 1790 at the age of 87 he preached twice in Northwich during his last preaching tour.

After he died in 1791 the Methodist Church was organised for the first time with Northwich as the centre of Cheshire's third Methodist circuit in 1792. Services had to be held at 7 am and 6 pm as they were not allowed at the same time as Anglican worship (10.30 am and 2 pm). Worshippers travelled long distances carrying candle lanterns. In the 1860s, following the introduction of gas lights, Anglicans introduced evening services because so many attended Methodist worship.

In 1833 Samuel Sugden was appointed Superintendent Minister of the Northwich Circuit. He was described as 'a man upon whose physical structure and mental calibre nature had not been lavish'. After the Methodist Conference of 1834 meetings were held in Crown Street Chapel, discussing moves to give more power to the congregation rather than the minister. Sugden was not invited. He expelled those who attended and dozens of others from the Methodist Church. Others withdrew in protest, 930 out of a membership of 1,600 during just three months. By March the situation was so bad that preachers were expelled and replaced so the two preachers fought to get into one pulpit.

Most of those expelled joined the informal Wesleyan Association which had caused the disagreements at the Conference. On 10 May 1835 they published their own preaching plan, listing places, times of alternative services at which one of the 19 expelled ministers would preach. It was the first rival plan ever issued. A new denomination emerged by this action in Northwich, formalised as the United Methodist Free Churches, by a meeting in Manchester in 1835.

The same year a wooden building called the Tabernacle was erected on the spot on Baron's Quay where Wesley preached, as their first chapel. Ten years later it was moved to stand near the junction of Witton Street and Timber Lane. When a brick chapel was built in 1854 it was retained behind.

During the early years of Methodism and Dissent and later of the Free Church, services were held in cottage kitchens or barns. Eventually these congregations attracted others to build a chapel.

Lostock and Hartford Anglican Churches were established after Methodist congregations were founded, arousing fears that the entire village would become Methodist. Hartford's Methodist services were held in the cottage of John Moores, a shoemaker. The first chapel was built in 1833 for £25 5s 9¾d.

Hartford Church was built by subscription, with the blessing of the Bishop of Chester. George Okell, Curate of Witton, objected as the new church would take away part of his living. To prevent this, double fees were charged for weddings etc, one for the Hartford Minister and one as compensation to Okell. That small church was replaced by the present church, designed by John Douglas of Sandiway in 1873.

Lostock Gralam Church was built in 1844 and Barnton Church in 1842; Rev Richard Greenall gave £1,000 to each. One of the brewing family, he provided funds to found several Anglican churches between Warrington and Northwich.

Holy Trinity, Castle was one of three built by the Weaver Navigation Trustees in 1842 by Act of Parliament. No movement was allowed on the River on Sunday and these 'watermen's churches' provided free seating no matter where the home was. Castle became a parish in 1929.

Leftwich, in Davenham parish, became more populated than Davenham. St Paul's Church was built in 1849 by Colonel Marshall, at the Chesterway/London Road junction. It was taken down in 1908 because of subsidence and replaced by a timber structure (now a pharmacy) until the parish was dissolved in 1931. It was succeeded by the Farm of the Good Shepherd on the site of Leftwich Hall when the estate was built in 1955.

Catholic worship was re-established in the early 19th century by Irish workers who took over the Crown Street Chapel. The present church was erected in 1866 in a typical Victorian group with the schools and priest's house.

Northwich played an interesting part in the history of the Salvation Army. Brass bands were popular with Victorian working classes. In 1878 Charles White suggested they should be used for street services. Salisbury was first, followed within months by Coventry and Northwich.

'Tin Missions' — prefabricated corrugated iron chapels — could be purchased in the 19th century. One was used by Baptists in Anderton and one was erected in Winnington by Anglicans in 1844. It was replaced in brick by Brunner Mond in 1897.

From 1880 a group assembled in an old smithy in Leicester Street following the Blue Ribbon Army, an evangelical movement. They purchased the Winnington Tin Mission and erected it on the site of the smithy. During the rebuilding the temperance group met in an outbuiding of the George and Dragon. Fire broke out during a meeting (which sounds like retribution!) They held open air services with a brass band. Some converts became missionaries, going to China, India and the West Indies. During a redevelopment in 1979 they moved to Leftwich.

One unusual preacher deserves a mention: James Crawford (or Crawfoot), 'The Man of the Forest' was influenced by the Primitive Methodist Church founded by James Clowes and Hugh Bourne at an outdoor camp meeting on Mow Cop in 1807. That year they visited him at his home near Dalefords Lane, Sandiway, and appointed him the first Primitive Methodist travelling minister anywhere, earning 10s per week. He was an elderly out of work farm labourer, needing the money to survive. Many followers were addressed at open-air gatherings aimed at reviving the enthusiasm of the early church. Things started to go wrong because he experimented with 'magic mushrooms'. Worshippers at his meetings experienced visions of angels and Bible figures as a result. They took the commandment to love their neighbour too literally and Mary Dunnet was revealed to have three living husbands. Crawford was called The Rustic Mystic until he and his Magic Methodists were unchurched in 1813.

After years of division the Methodist Conference agreed to unite in 1932, but it was not until the 1950s that shortage of ministers forced three circuits to unite. The Wesleyans were administered from London Road Chapel, the United Free Church from the Central Chapel (by Timber Lane) and the Primitive Methodists from the Bourne Chapel in Station Road. All three chapels have since been demolished.

As demoninations move closer together two funeral chapels in Witton Cemetery stand silent witness to years of division. One was for Nonconformists, the other for Catholics, who were not allowed to hold funeral services in the church. They have become obsolete as motor hearses allow the service to take place at a great distance from the place of internment.

The Wesley Chest in Hartford Chapel was made from wood from Leftwich Chapel. (NC)

An Inland Port

The economic development of Northwich depended upon transport to take away salt and import fuel. Despite pioneering works the story is one of greed, jealousy and resistance to change.

Evidence of mediaeval transport is elusive, but routes into Derbyshire and North Wales have been identified from names including 'salt', 'salter' or 'white'. In the 17th century salt was taken by pack-horse to a warehouse at Pickering's Wharf, Acton Bridge, at the tidal limit beyond which large boats could not pass. Ox carts took salt to London.

By the 18th century 4,000 Cheshire families earned part of their living using horses, when not needed for farming. They took salt into coalfields, returning with coal taken for part-exchange to salt works.

Northwich was a stage-coach cross-roads, with the Crown, Crown and Anchor and Angel as staging posts where horses were changed while passengers took refreshments. They could change from the London — Warrington and the north routes to the one from York through Chester to Ireland *via* Holyhead. The Bull's Head, Davenham and the Black Greyhound, Lostock, served similar routes avoiding Northwich. It could take a day and half to reach London but usually took seven days, costing £5 around 1800 while a letter to London cost 10d. A daily coach to Runcorn met a ferry from Liverpool on the tide.

There are stories of highwaymen hiding in Winnington Woods and — most unlikely — of Dick Turpin hiding at Lostock. Edward Higgins, Knutsford's highwayman, danced with ladies, examining their jewels and helping himself as they returned home. He stopped Lady Warburton, returning to Arley, who recognised him, thinking it was a prank. He was hanged in 1767.

Samuel Thorley was hanged in 1777, for robbing the Northwich to Warrington mail-boy. Such riders carried mailbags until the last were replaced by passenger mail-coach, when Hartford Station opened in 1837. After five attempts at escaping from Chester Castle his body was exhibited in gibbet irons, hanging from a 50ft tall spiked pole on Helsby Hill, as a warning seen all over the district. It was removed on the first night.

In the 18th century the two Roman roads, with London Road and Penny's Lane, were improved by turnpike trusts, recouping costs by charging all who used them, adding to the costs of goods. Coal cost three shillings at Prescott but four times that by the time it reached Northwich.

Agitation to improve the river started in 1699 from rock salt mine owners led by Thomas Slyford. It was fiercely opposed by farmers and owners of mansions near the river, who were worried about intrusion and theft by boatmen. Sir George Warburton of Arley (as Cheshire MP) was persuaded of the benefits and became one of the chief subscribers, having at first opposed it. In 1720 Parliament approved navigation of the Weaver and the Mersey, authorising eleven timber-sided locks between Winsford and Pickering's, constructed in

1721. The first barge — carrying 45 tons of salt — left Northwich on 1 January 1722. Carriage of salt was reduced from 18 shillings a ton to three. Timber locks were replaced by stone in 1760.

The Act approved navigation of the Dane to Middlewich and in 1724 allowed extension to Nantwich, because of opposition from those towns whose industry was threatened. Neither started, though plans to extend to Nantwich were revived in 1955 and the Dane was navigable up to the weir above Marshall's Salt Works. Witton Brook was also navigable for a short distance. The Weaver has the longest proportion of its length navigable for sea-going vessels of any river in the world.

In 1757 the Sankey Brook Canal provided a link to transport Lancashire coal to the salt works in barges. The river navigations provided outlets to export Lancashire and Cheshire products *via* Liverpool, showing the advantages of water transport. They influenced the Duke of Bridgewater to build his canal in 1759, linking coal mines at Worsley to Manchester and later to Runcorn.

The same year Metcalf's salt mine under Northwich Lock collapsed, destroying it. As an emergency measure a dam was built. It prevented direct shipment of goods from Winsford, which had to be unloaded and carried to boats waiting on the other side of the dam. This inhibited Winsford's development, giving Northwich the competitive edge for the next decade.

One horse pulled a barge containing more than what two hundred horses could carry. The Weaver flats could use sail, or four to six people sometimes replaced one horse.

These successes prompted Midland manufacturers to construct a canal, authorised in 1766, joining the Mersey and the Humber. Their leader was Josiah Wedgewood, the potter, who needed salt for glazes. They intended to link with the Weaver at Northwich and to dig an extension to Burton on the Wirral, avoiding port costs at Liverpool.

The Duke of Bridgewater did not want to lose monopoly of access to the Mersey and arranged for the Trent and Mersey to join his canal at Preston Brook, using his locks. The economy of this was farcical compared to the costs of tunnels at Saltersford, Barnton and Preston Brook. Runcorn locks were inadequately time-consuming and barges had to pay additional fees to use the Duke's canal and locks. Hold-ups were caused as the tunnels were only wide enough for one barge.

They were dug from opposite ends by navvies (navigators) working inwards causing 'dog-legs'. In the 400 feet long Saltersford Tunnel at one point it is impossible to see light at either end. Horses walked over the top while men lay on their backs and 'legged' the barge through, with their feet on the tunnel roof. Children waited by the tunnels in the hope of earning a farthing doing this.

The Barnton Town Brook records expenses of a coroner's inquest on a man killed digging the tunnel. An industrial area developed there with a rope-walk, clogger and a general shop. The first shopkeeper was transported to Australia for stealing from the boatees.

The Duke ensured that the canal was kept away from Northwich, providing an alternative route for salt making, away from the town in Wincham, Marston, Anderton and Barnton. Wharves developed at Wincham and Broken Cross, where the canal broke through a cross roads. Goods were carried from them to a warehouse by the Dane Bridge by horse. Barges on the Dane also loaded and unloaded goods from the warehouse.

Ill-feeling between the Duke and the Weaver Navigation Trustees prevented Northwich becoming an important canal centre. The Duke killed plans by the second Thomas Marshall for a canal from Northwich through Knutsford, Mottram St Andrew (a cattle market), Macclesfield and Stockport to Manchester. Silk was carried to Macclesfield from the Dane Bridge Warehouse by pack-horse. Marshall hoped to develop trade in silk and cotton as well as salt and coal.

James Brindley, the canal engineer, avoided locks, following the contours of the land. The canal came to the crest of the Weaver Valley at Anderton. From 1788 the Navigation Trustees purchased land between the two waterways for salt from Middlewich and pottery from North Staffordshire to be taken downhill. By 1800 a basin was constructed, allowing river-boats to get closer to the embankment. Two wooden chutes were built overhanging the basin, for salt unloaded from narrowboats on the canal to be tipped into boats below; hence the nick-name 'The Tip' for the Stanley Arms.

Although it added to labour costs it avoided holds-up at the tunnels, Runcorn Locks saving the tolls for using the Bridgewater canal. An inclined plane was built with two railway lines, along which trucks worked as counter-balances, pulling each other other up the opposite line. Crates of pottery went down while china clay and other goods went up. Loss or revenue caused the Duke to persuade Parliament to forbid transhipment of anything but salt. This was repealed in 1825 when a second entrance to the basin opened with a third chute and another inclined plane. An Act of 1872 authorised construction of a boat-lift, designed by Edwin Clarke and opened in 1875. By the end of the century 38,000 tons of salt were tipped down the chutes and 190,000 tons of traffic passed through the lift each year.

When built it used hydraulic power; the weight of one caisson going down forced liquid through pipes, causing the other to rise. By 1908 the pipes had rusted and were replaced by an electrically operated system, with metal cables passing over pulleys to suspended cast — iron counter-weights. The chutes ceased to be used in the 1950s and the lift was closed by 1984 because of corroded supports.

The Weaver Navigation was improved in 1875 by their engineer, Edward Leader Williams. He improved the locks, reducing them to just five, built in pairs. One took a narrow-boat but the other at 228 feet long by 42 feet took four narrowboats or one steamer. As a result of these designs and his work on the lift, he was employed to design and build the Manchester Ship Canal using similar locks.

Town Bridge was too low and the arches too narrow for large vessels. Masts had to be lowered for flat-boats to pass under it. In 1858 the stone bridge was demolished and replaced by a steel one 15 feet 10 inches above water. Subsidence averaged 4½ inches a year until Parliament authorised two swing bridges in 1893. The new Hayhurst bridge was provided 600 feet upstream ensuring there was always one crossing available.

They were designed by Colonel John Saner, Chief Engineer of the Weaver Navigation. The Hayhurst was the first, costing £16,687 17s 3d. It opened on 1 September 1899, named after the Navigation Chairman. They were designed to overcome problems from subsidence as floating structures not connected to the land in any way. Most of the weight (225 tons) is carried on a cylindrical caisson under the west end of each bridge.

To act as a cantilever the superstructure is higher on that side with cast-iron weights suspended underneath. These could be added or reduced in number allowing adjustments to maintain a level road. Each caisson is enclosed within a chamber of wooden piling to prevent freezing. The bridge is turned by steel ropes operated by an electric motor. The swing-bridges were the first to be operated by electricity.

The old girder bridge was moved upsteam intact on narrow-boats and re-opened as the Victoria Bridge, providing a new crossing for the Dane as part of a new road to the Hayhurst Bridge.

The Grand Junction, the first cross-country railway, passed two miles from Northwich in 1837 with a station at Hartford. Lord Stallbridge, Chairman of the Railway Company, built a house at Heyeswood by the station; for his convenience the London Glasgow and Cornwall trains stopped there — as they still do. Hartford is still served by Intercity trains. Until Crewe was linked to Manchester and Chester, post and passengers used Hartford, completing the journey by stage-coach.

A Methodist minister at this period was travelling to Hartford to marry in Whitegate, when a fire was started by a spark from the engine, igniting luggage carried on the top of the passenger waggons. Soldiers climbed on the roofs to extinguish the flames and one was killed as the train passed under a bridge. The Minister promptly started a campaign which resulted in the invention of the communication cord.

The stations were kept away from Winsford and Northwich as the Navigation Trustees were concerned at this threat to their trade. A similar concern affected the Cheshire Lines Company building the line from Manchester to Chester. A meeting at the Crown in 1858 aimed to raise local investment. Shopkeepers were convinced that the railway would cause everyone to shop in Manchester, ruining Northwich and nothing was raised. The line opened to Northwich on 1 January 1863. Then the viaduct extended it to Helsby in 1869, reaching Chester in 1874. The foundations of the arches rest on cotton bales to cushion them on the wet valley floor. The Navigation insisted that the metal section above the river be high enough for sailing vessels to pass under.

As competing companies were responsible, a joint station for transferring between journeys was not considered or Hartford could have developed as a small version of Crewe. The Cheshire Lines Company was established as an attempt to invade the area of the London North Western in 1865 as a link between four rival companies. Most of the lines were in Lancashire and lines were the only thing they owned. Rolling stock from the owning companies ran along them.

Marshalling lines existed around Northwich Station. There were pens for cattle auctions and stables for heavy horses, which hauled road-wagons taking goods to their destinations. With freight trains from each company and ICI's own stock the Station was a haunt of train-spotters; rolling stock from Northwich had the identity 8E.

Branch-lines were built into the works. Brunner Mond imported vast quantities of limestone from Buxton using their own rolling stock. The last rail link was the 'Dodger' to Sandbach and Lawton *via* Middlewich. It was never successful for passengers, but carried coal and salt.

Motorised road transport for freight developed after the First World War, when the military sold surplus vehicles. Local haulage contractors prospered by carrying Brunner Mond products.

The ever-growing volume of motor traffic saw the town Centre pedestrianised in the 1960s, with new roads bypassing it and poor housing replaced by car-parks. The volume of rail freight has reduced while canal freight ended after the paralysing Big Freeze of 1963. After this Northwich Pond was lined with many narrowboats awaiting conversion to be used as holiday vessels. ICI sold their river fleet in 1979. Today commercial potential for Northwich includes proximity to the M6, the Hartford rail link to London, and the proximity to Manchester International Airport.

ABOVE: Pack horse train: most were less impressive, using farm horses.
(ICI) BELOW: Horse-drawn omnibus at the Greyhound, Lostock,
carried passengers to stations or markets. (NC)

ABOVE: Designs for the Weaver Locks in 1875 secured Leader Williams the job of designing the Manchester Ship Canal. (AH) LEFT: Vale Royal 'Cut' shows the straight, Navigation and the winding 'Old River'. (AH) RIGHT: Sluices near the Edwardian Sewage Pumping Station in Dock Road help control flood waters.

ABOVE: Barnton, by R. Bolton, 1881, shows the 'Old River', the Navigation and a canal barge approaching the tunnel. (JGS) LEFT: Flat-boats tied up on Sunday morning at Wallerscote. (ICI) RIGHT: A busy scene in the 1930s: barges pass from Hunt's Lock under the viaduct. (NC)

ABOVE: Two-masted coastal vessel at Winnington Wharf. (ICI)
BELOW: The ICI steam barges, Winnington, 1974. (ICI)

ABOVE: Launching one of ICI's steamers sideways into the river. (NC)
BELOW: The *Athelbrae*, a 158ft long tanker, was the largest vessel; built at Yarwood's in 1954-5. (DG)

ABOVE: Boat building shed with two slip-ways to repair two narrowboats. (NC) BELOW: Narrowboats heading for Bourneville at Lostock. (NC) INSET: Date plaque with carving of the hull of a Weaver flat-boat, Navigation Road. (SP)

ABOVE: Narrowboats at Barnton in the 'Big Freeze' of 1963 which ended the commercial use of canals. (NC) BELOW: Vale Royal Viaduct and the Cutting at Hartford (constructed in 1837) from prints of 1854.

ABOVE: Northwich Station, 1917: an early motor-car stands among the carriages waiting for passengers. (MH) CENTRE: Cheshire Lines shunters risked lives using hooked poles to join wagons up in the marshalling yards. (NC) BELOW: The Northwich Terminus confirmed Northwich as the central area for shopping in Mid-Cheshire. (NC)

ABOVE: The establishment of 'bus services made it possible to establish out-of-town estates. (NC) CENTRE: Lunchtime at Harris's Depôt, Lostock, 1956. (JC) BELOW: The stone Town Bridge built in 1662; this print was made 'for the benefit of poor and retired Flat-men to find them tobacco when hard up'. (CL)

ABOVE: The girder Town Bridge built in 1858 was moved intact on narrowboats to become the Victoria Bridge. (NC) BELOW: The swing bridge authorised in 1883; the baskets were to signal between the bridges. (NC)

ABOVE: Town Bridge is open here to allow barges to pass through. (MH) BELOW: Colonel Sayner's drawing of the bridge shows the floating air chamber and cantilever weights.

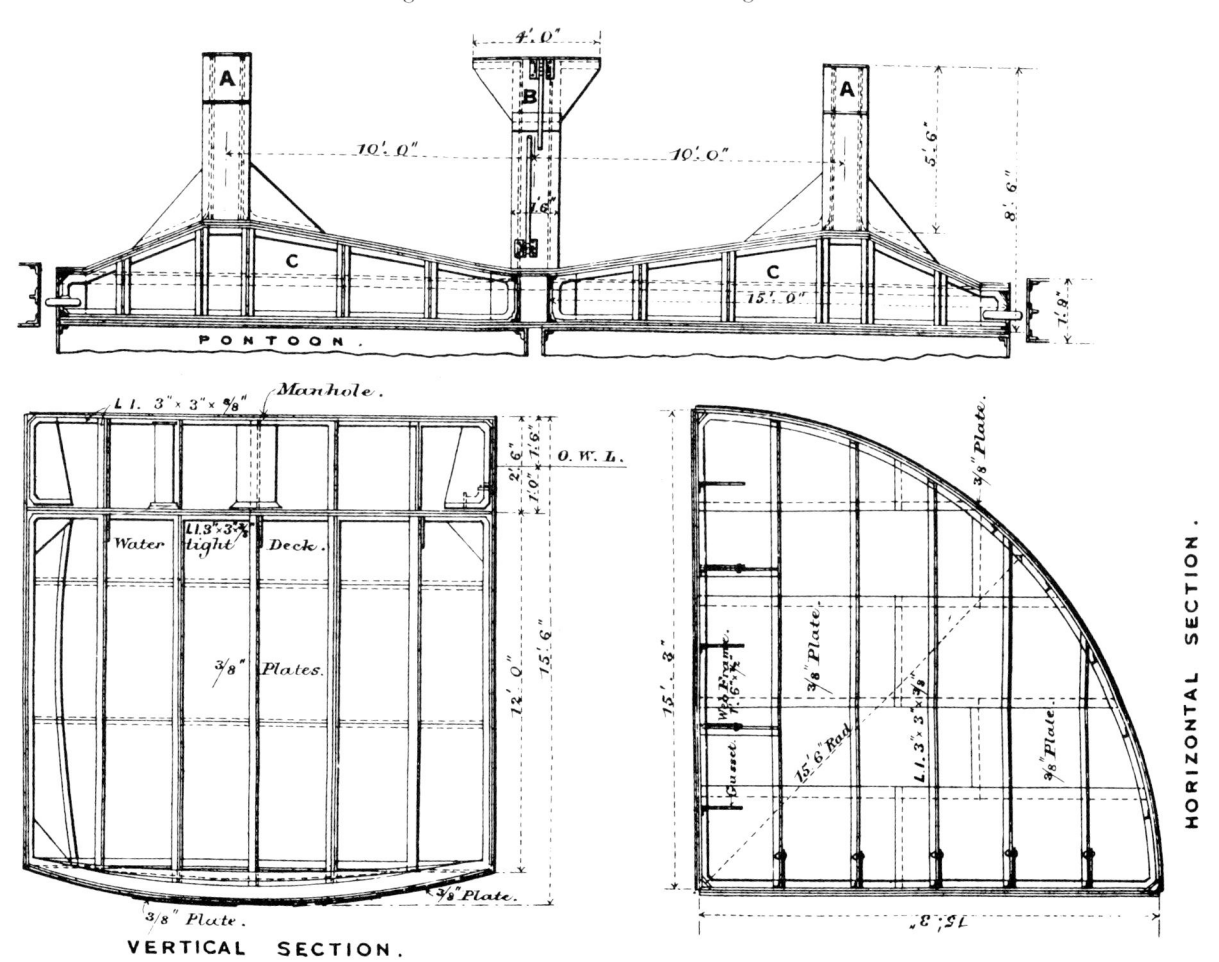

VERTICAL SECTION.

HORIZONTAL SECTION.

LEFT: Dane Bridge in 1891 was high enough for the Victoria Bridge to be taken under it. (CL) RIGHT: By 1977 subsidence had lowered the town centre so that high water flowed over the foot-way. (NC) BELOW: Winnington Swing Bridge from a post-card posted in 1904. (MH)

ABOVE: Hartford stone bridge, 1907. BELOW: Hartford steel bridge, built in 1939, took traffic around Northwich using the by-pass.

The Anderton lift originally used hydraulic power and was flanked by tips down which salt was transferred from the canal. ABOVE: The lift was converted to an electric system in 1908, using numerous wheels and pulleys. (NC)

The Curse of the Country

Schoolchildren might agree with the sentiment expresed in 1883 to the Northwich School Attendance Committee by John Sutton of the Golden Square, Hartford. Accused of not sending his children to school he said 'Between ourselves Gentlemen, Education is the curse of the country. It is the cause of one half of the prisons being filled with crime and craft. It is the worst thing that ever came to this country'. When ordered to send them to school 'he left the room flourishing his arms and declaring against the characteristics of the age'. Like many people of his era he believed that 'children should be earning not learning'.

Others, however, believed in the value of education and there is a long and significant history of education in Northwich. There might have been some teaching during the Middle Ages with tuition from the clergy. No records have survived but a Schoolmaster's Lane is recorded as early as 1536.

The recorded story of education locally dates from the Renaissance. Sir John Deane was a son of Laurence Deane of Surlach. As he was presented for ordination by Vale Royal Abbey in 1519, he may have been taught there. He became Vicar of St Bartholomew's parish, London, in 1540 and kept contact with relatives in Northwich. The title 'Sir' was used instead of 'Rev'. He was not a knight. He endowed a Grammar School in Witton Churchyard in 1558. Among the regulations he ordered that 'a week before Christmas and Easter, according to the old custom, they barr and keep forth the schoolmaster, in such sort as other scholars doe in great schools'. This was to mark a vacation, not to cause him offence. He specified that they should practise, 'with their bowes and arrowes only' during the vacations and 'eschewe all bowleing, carding, dyceing, quoiteinge, and all other unlawful games'.

It appears that Deane provided an endowment for a school as John Bracegirdle (he used several spellings) was already teaching there. Bracegirdle had an Oxford MA and became the first Perpetual Curate of Witton (still part of Great Budworth Parish) in 1548. He leased a house by the churchyard from Sir Thomas Venables, Lord of the Manor. He then added to the meagre stipend of a curate by charging for teaching in the house. He was Vicar of Budworth from 1558 to 1561, keeping responsibility for Witton. It might have been this move which prompted Deane to provide funds to continue the work. Bracegirdle moved, to become Vicar of Stratford on Avon where, in 1564, he baptised Shakespeare.

Among his pupils at Witton was John Brownsword, who became a schoolmaster. He followed Bracegirdle to Stratford as master of the Grammar School before becoming master at Macclesfield. His memorial there records him as 'The first of poets, the leader of the grammarians, and the flower of schoolmasters'. He published books of poems in Latin which were considered to be outstanding at the time. It was believed that Shakespeare was a pupil of Brownsword but he left Stratford shortly after Bracegirdle died in 1565.

It was claimed that Deane also founded Great Budworth Grammar School which was in existence as early as 1563 with James Roe as schoolmaster. John Bruen of Stapleford attended it and became the best known of Cheshire's Puritan gentry, to whom others sent their children for instruction.

Robert Clive of India and General Woolfe were pupils at a school kept by Dr Eaton, variously described as at Lostock and Allostock in the 1730s. Both had dissenting chapels and Clive stayed with the Minister at Allostock. The story that Clive was the leader of a group of boys, who terrorised shopkeepers into giving them money or goods by threatening to break windows and steal goods, sounds as if Lostock was the more likely location.

In 1768 Thomas Kaye left his house and land in trust for the education of six poor children from Witton and six from Northwich. The house became the Queen's Head Inn, though the rent was still used for education. Witton Grammar School also received the rent from the Saracen's Head Inn at Chester.

In the mid-19th century the wife of Thomas Marshall, the salt proprietor, provided a reading room at Hartford, which was incorporated into Thorn Cottage. He gave adult classes in the 3 Rs and penny readings (the price included a bowl of soup) from newspapers and periodicals to villagers there when newspapers and periodicals were expensive ways of spreading news and information. There was a small reading room near to the Town Bridge and by the 1850s an Institute existed in Timber Lane, providing adult classes and a reading room.

The Methodists maintained Sunday Schools. In the early 19th century they provided elementary teaching in reading and writing on the one day away from work for church members of all ages. The little Wesleyan Sunday School in London Road was built in 1783. It is now used by a hairdresser, but is the oldest school building in the town. The United Methodist Chapel built in 1854 at the junction of Timber Lane and Witton Streets had a Sunday School in the basement for 500 pupils.

The Weaver Navigation Trustees maintained a school close to their offices from the 1820s. This was linked to schools in Winsford and Runcorn for children of families working on the river. The facilities allowed children to go to any of the schools if their parents needed to take them to help on the boats. The Tythe Map records the 'Brat House' by the school!

This contrasts with problems of children on the canals. Brunner encouraged the setting up of one of the first branches of the NSPCC outside London. Their inspectors at the turn of the century commented on children who reached school-leaving age without ever entering one. Others attended at a different school each day as parents moved about the country. As soon as an inspector appeared near the canal, children kept away from school to work on the boats were hidden in the cargo or sent running along the tow-path to warn others.

The National School was set up in 1813 in Witton Street, which provided elementary education for the poor with places for over 1,000 children. In 1815 there were reported to be 26 day schools held in private houses in the parish (*sic*) of Witton. Thomas Hand was appointed Master of Witton Grammar School in 1822, coming into conflict with the Trustees. From the earliest days an Usher had provided elementary education for poor children in the upstairs school room. Hand believed this downgraded the school and wanted to develop an upper class grammar school as he took in boarders from other areas, charging rent to stay at his house.

Matters came to a head when Thomas Jones was appointed Usher. Jones was a Dissenter and as enthusiastic about free education for the poor as Hand was about an upper class boarding school teaching Latin grammar. Jones filled the upper room with 120 of 'the roughest lot of youths ever brought together'. It was a real ragged school with pupils in clogs or bare feet. Hand locked them out but the trustees changed the lock. Obviously the wealthy would not pay for their sons to be educated in the same building. The case went to law and was heard in Chancery from 1834 to 1850. It was ordered that a grammar school and a lower school were to continue and admission was to be open to anyone in the Chapelry for the fee of 4d. Elementary Latin was to be taught in the lower school to encourage pupils to progress to the grammar school.

There were various private academies during the 19th century and two music teachers were recorded in 1860. One of the most outstanding schools of the period was Winnington Hall Seminary, operating in the 1860s, described as 'a first-class educational establishment for young ladies'. Miss Margaret Bell, the headmistress and proprietor, was a forceful woman with advanced views on the education of girls. Good manners, deportment and lady-like skills of embroidery and painting were taught. Winnington girls were expected to achieve good academic levels. In addition they played ball games and were even permitted to climb trees. This shocked visitors as they wore crinolines, revealing more than was demure when up a tree!

She took girls to concerts in Manchester and invited Sir Charles Hallé to visit Winnington. He became a regular visitor to the school along with John Ruskin, the first Professor of Fine Art at Oxford and leader of Victorian artistic taste. In 1859 he wrote to his father 'this is such a nice place that I am going to stay till Monday; an enormous old fashioned house — full of galleries and up and down stairs — but with magnificent large rooms where wanted: the drawing room is a huge octagon — like the tower of a castle . . . in the evening brightly lighted, with groups of girls scattered round it, it is quite a beautiful scene in its way'. He commented about their chapel and described the joy of hearing Hallé playing the piano for the girls.

He gave drawing lessons to the girls and wrote to them frequently. 'The Winnington Letters of John Ruskin' have been published, and are written in the most sentimental terms, reading like love letters.

After the school moved from Winnington in 1868 Ruskin lost one of the few places where he was comfortable and after an unfortunate affair with a young girl called Rose la Touche he lost his sanity.

There were several Dame Schools in the area, including one in Barnton kept by Mary Coates, a widow who had been the mistress of John Marshall. She was known as an alcoholic and used her fees to buy drink.

Compulsory education was provided for children under the age of 13 by the Act of 1870, though it was not until 1891 that it was required to be free. A local schoolboard was appointed, becoming the forerunner of the Urban District Council, with the power to levy rates. It purchased the Manor of Northwich, using the revnue from the market to support schools and provide free places for the poor.

It was responsible for administering the following elementary schools in 1900: Victoria Road, just opened, costing £14,000 for 300 boys, 300 girls and 200 infants — it replaced three temporary schools; Castle Girls School, founded in 1805 and included an infants school; St Paul's, Danebridge, built by Colonel Marshall in 1853 by the entrance to the Drill Field; Witton Boys School, founded in 1817 and moved to the Church Walk building in 1896; Timber Lane School, built in 1881 and notable for the timber paved road outside to stop the noise of vehicles from the timber yard disturbing lessons. Witton also had an infants school while the Weaver Navigation and Catholic Schools were for 'mixed and infants'.

As ever in the story of Northwich during the second quarter of the 19th century, John Brunner played a major part, serving as chairman of the Education Committee for many years. He provided an elementary school at Winnington in 1885 as an essential part of the factory community. The company management retained control of the Board of Governors until a new school was built in 1985, when it was only company-controlled school in the country.

It was a non-denominational school. One of Brunner's major political aims was for schools independent of churches, and in this he often crossed the Bishop of Chester. Bishop Jayne asked him not to build the school so that pupils would attend church schools. Brunner took no notice and, when he extended the school in 1892, he pointed out that many children from nonconformist families travelled from Barnton and even further to attend. With Ellis, his election assistant, he published a book on education in Cheshire, recording the situation in the 1890s, and served as Chairman of the Local School Board.

The Education Act of 1902 abolished the Local Board, passing authority to Cheshire County Council as the Local Education Authority.

In 1903 Witton Grammar School was criticised for its outmoded teaching. The Board of Education Inspector criticised the private school background of the master and said the two assistants were insufficient. A Girls' High School had been founded in 1890 in buildings leased from Ludwig Mond. This experienced difficulties after girls were admitted on County Scholarships. The parents of fee-paying girls transferred them to private schools. Brunner proposed to build a new school for secondary education. He was determined that it should be co-educational and nondenominational. After some resistance the old Grammer School merged into the new and the name of Sir John Deane was revived, although Brunner might have been more appropriate. The third school building became the Council House. Brunner Mond introduced compulsory evening 'continuation classes' for boy employees in 1889, held at Winnington School. It was apparent that attending school after a full day's work was tiring, especially for younger boys. When the 1918 Education Act allowed day classes for 14- to 16-year-olds Brunner Mond became pioneers of day-release training at Winnington School.

After the Second World War the introduction of Primary, Secondary Modern and Grammar Schools and raising of the school-leaving age to 15 saw the elementary schools become primary schools. Secondary modern schools were built at Hartford and Rudheath. A girls' Grammar School was established at Leftwich. These are now Comprehensive Schools and Sir John Deane's is a VIth Form College.

OPPOSITE: The rent from the Queen's Head paid to educate poor children. (CL) ABOVE: The Northwich Board of Education used rooms in the Talbot. (NC) BELOW: The 18th century Witton Grammar School, on the site of John Bracegirdle's house.

ABOVE: Laundry class at Barnton Brunner School. (CM) BELOW: First aid instruction, ICI apprentices training, 1960s. (ICI)

More than a Pinch of Salt

In the 19th century salt manufacture reached gigantic proportions around Northwich, with vast factories. Availability of brine or rock salt over a wide area resulted in a liberal scattering of works unlike the concentration by the river in Winsford. The railway branch lines and canal provided alternatives to river transport. Parts of the Dane and Wade Brook were navigable with wharves and salt works along them.

Because of the corrosive action of salt, brick and nails were avoided as much as possible in the construction of salt works and warehouses. They had plank walls supported by outside joists, rather like vertical floor-boards.

Salt works were arranged in two sections; the pan-houses where the brine was boiled and the hot houses where the salt was dried. Above the pans the apex of the roof was open to allow steam to escape. The stoke holes were at one end of the pan and flues carried the heat in ducts underneath, then under an adjoining 'hot-house'. There the hot air was ducted through more brickwork, which became hot, and blocks of fine salt were stacked to slowly dry and harden to a brick-like state. Above were lofts where salt was crushed and bagged.

Two types of salt were made, although each had variants depending on the ultimate use. The time that brine was heated for and the temperature to which it was raised created different sized crystals. Short rapid boiling produced small fine grains; long slow simmering produced large cubic crystals. Traditional additives including egg-white, ox-blood and soft-soap formed different qualities. Human urine was passed directly into the pans to clear froth. Common salt was taken direct from the pans and piled on the wooden floors — called hurdles — by the pan-side. Excess moisture drained between the gaps in the planks. The coarse salt was used in industrial processes such as curing fish or meat and for pottery glazes. It was removed on two wheeled hand-carts along jetties over-hanging the canal, river or railway and tipped into barges or trucks below. It was stored in river and canal-side warehouses — some of incredible size. Sloping sites were selected; they were built with a full facade facing the water at the front, with a loading door in the gable of the roof entered from the bank. Salt was tipped in at the top from the bank and loaded from the bottom of the tip.

The process for making fine salts was more complex. Salt crystals were drawn to the side of the pan, using the long-handled rake. Salt was scooped from the pan using a 'skimmer' with a spade-like handle but a metal disc pierced with holes as the blade. Salt was tipped into elm-wood tubs which rested on long iron bars suspended like a shelf on the inside of the pan, called 'dogs'. The labourer placed one tub onto the dogs, filled it, and then placed the next one by its side, moving along the pan.

Each tub had holes in the bottom to let surplus moisture drain away. The tubs were then upturned onto the plank floor and something resembling a tall rectangular sand-castle was turned out. It dried quickly because of the heat and could be carefully lifted onto a hand-cart to be moved into the hot-house for the 'stoving' process which hardened it to a brick-like block. These could be cut to size and sold as a block though usually, after all this setting and drying, they were ground down to form fine-grained table or cooking salts. Much was put into stout cotton bags over two feet tall and a foot wide for export to Africa, where they were often made into children's clothes. When the trade to Nigeria ended in the 1980s following wars, bags were in use with trade-marks of works which closed a century before, as Nigerians would only buy bags with recognised marks. Such salt was known as Lagos after Nigeria's chief port.

Early mines followed the bell-pit arrangement. The Northwich brewers, Sandifords, used a diagram of one as a trade mark. From a central shaft miners excavated outwards in all directions, creating a circular mine. At first they were in the top bed and most eventually flooded.

This did not mean failure for the proprietors, who simply switched to pumping brine from the flooded mine until this caused the ground to subside. An example of a flooded and collapsed mine is the Adalaide at Marston, where a small part of the submerged pumping engine can be seen above the surface of the flash. The collapsed mines owned by the Swiss proprietors Neumans and the Liverpool merchant Nicholas Ashton (who also owned coal mines at St Helen's) can be seen by the Warrington Road. The flashes are now filled with lime waste.

The Great Marston Mine was a Victorian tourist attraction. The most famous visitor was Grand Duke Nicholas of Russia (not the Tsar as is often claimed) who was entertained underground by the British Association. The buffet table was decorated with flowers and wax candles (smelly tallow ones were used by miners). Visitors commented about mice living in it, taken down in hay for the pit ponies. 'At every step flashes of broken light gleam from the floor or are glanced from the sparry roof and it is easy to imagine that we are treading the pearly streets of some enchanter's hall'.

Visits to the mines were popular; Baron's Quay Mine charged people for admission, raising more than £1,000 which was donated to local churches to repair subsidence damage. The Adalaide Mine had a famous ballroom at the bottom of the shaft, where social events were held.

Herman Falk, a German with works at Winsford, introduced steam barges in 1863 to break the power of the Flatmen's Association, formed in 1792 before the Combinations Act. Although described as a 'friendly society', it was one of the earliest trade unions. Boats were tied to a table of charges to protect against exploitation by proprietors. Falk side-stepped this by introducing steam vessels.

During the 19th century the price for salt varied greatly. When prices were high 'small masters' set up. By undercutting prices they created a slump. Using family labour they offered lower prices than proprietors who employed labour. When prices fell they went out of business. To counter this in 1872 a group of Manchester businessmen unsuccessfully proposed a limited company to control all salt making. In 1888 when prices were extremely low Falk successfully reintroduced the idea, forming the Salt Union — the first industrial cartel. Salt proprietors presented a price for all their works, boats etc, which were purchased in exchange for shares in the new Company. It aimed to close unprofitable works. As all former owners had a share of the Company's profits none should suffer loss. However, opportunities for workers were greatly reduced.

The Union never succeeded in its aims and almost at once there were rivalries among shareholders. Instead of reducing prices, they increased them so that rival works opened, undercutting prices again. Worse was to come in 1892.

The Union took control of virtually all salt-moving vessels on the Weaver. They introduced working hours which made no allowance for sleep. The boatmen struck and the Union retaliated, taking seven men to court who were on their vessels but refused to work. The JPs were all Union shareholders, but the case was withdrawn as the law under which they were prosecuted applied to sea-going vessels.

When the Union employed men to replace strikers the saltworkers struck in support. On 25 August the *Cynosure*, pulling the *Antelope*, was showered with missiles for half a mile. As it neared Northwich, an angry crowd followed, growing larger until the engineer leapt ashore, abandoning the vessels. The blackleg crew was returned to Liverpool by train.

Two days later a barge left Liverpool with an escort of four police officers, who left the vessel at Winnington Bridge, handing over to the Northwich police. On the river-bank angry people showered the barge with bricks and stones. It was damaged in Saltersford Lock and ran aground.

The bitter dispute continued for a violent month until the Bishop of Chester and High Sheriff arbitrated. The watermen agreed to pay the blacklegs £500 for loss of earnings, all were reinstated and hours of work were reduced to acceptable times. The Salt Union was absorbed by ICI in 1933, having failed to establish the monopoly for salt making it intended. Today brine from Northwich is pumped to be processed at Weston Point, Runcorn, on the Ship Canal for loading onto ships. This is less costly than transporting finished salt, off-loading and reloading. It echoes 18th century trade in rock salt to works on the Mersey. A pipe on the railway bridge also carries Northwich brine to Widnes chemical works.

The only salt made locally today is at the New Cheshire Works at Wincham. The Bates family firm employ 'multiple effect' technology, using vast enclosed vacuum tanks. Steam from the first is channelled into tubes in the next to heat the brine; steam from this heats the third container. All are made from Monel, a corrosion-resistant alloy. Salt is drawn from the bottom as slurry and dried. The technique was developed in America for manufacturing sugar.

Close to this, the most modern salt works in Europe, the Lion Salt Works is the last open-pan works in the country. It closed when demand from Nigeria ended and was purchased by Vale Royal Borough Council to be restored as a fully operational factory with visitor facilities and museum displays.

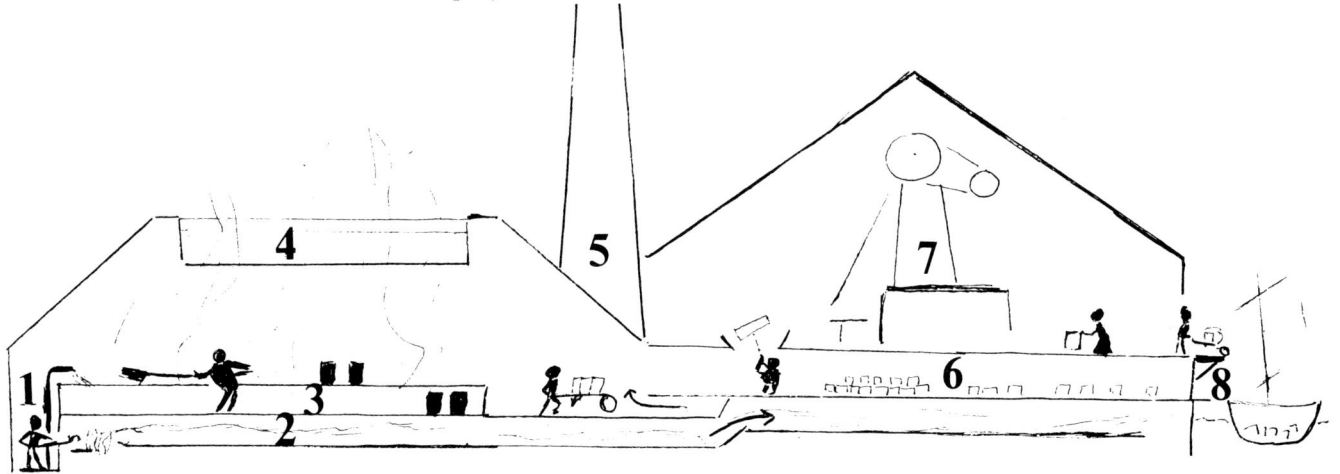

Cross-section of salt works: 1 stoke holes and brine pipe; 2 flue under pan; 3 pan with tubs; 4 open-topped roof; 5 chimney; 6 hot house; 7 crushing machine; 8 tipping into barge.

ABOVE: Crystals from common pans dry on the hurdle (wooden floor). (ICI) BELOW: Raking open-air pans; summer sun aided evaporation and winter cold slowed crystal formation. (ICI)

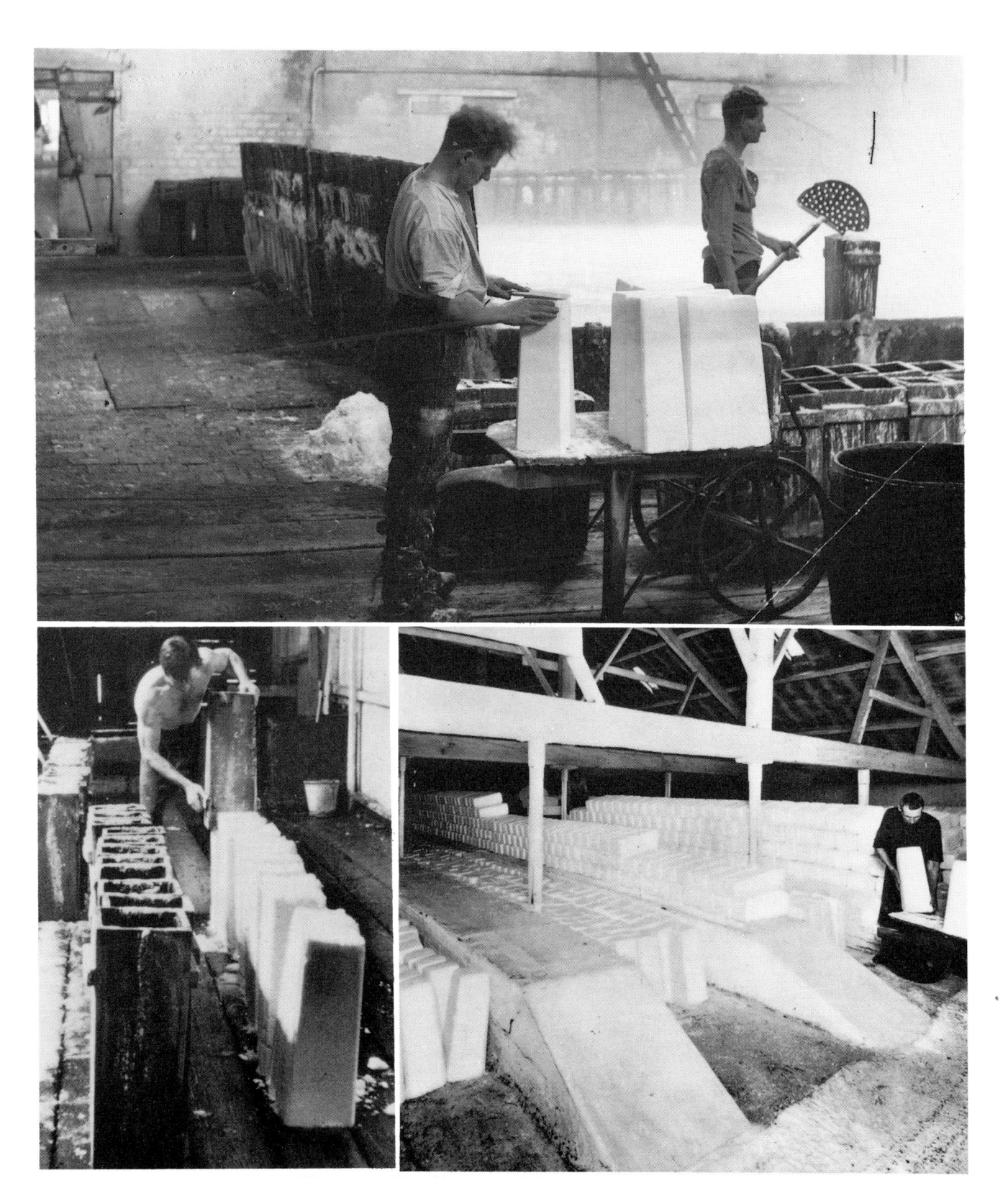

ABOVE: Filling tubs with a skimmer and shaping blocks with a happer; the barrel is to soak tools. (ICI) LEFT: Tipping fine salt from tubs. (ICI) RIGHT: Hot-house, where blocks were heated and dried over flues. (ICI)

ABOVE: Using spikes to lift blocks into the loft; note clogs and breeches.
(ICI) BELOW: Elegant visitors view a huge common salt warehouse
from overhead walk-ways. (CM)

ABOVE: Salt chutes to tip salt into flat boats at Anderton. (CM)
CENTRE: Card posted 1907 shows use of 'barrows' (baskets) with store shed and pan-side. (MH) BELOW: Massive warehouse for salt from barrows at the Lion Salt Works. (LS)

MR DICKINSON'S REPORT ON THE SALT DISTRICTS. 1882.

(TO FACE THE PART ON THE ROCK SALT MINES.)

SECTION SHOWING THE
METHOD BY WHICH THE TOP BED OF ROCK SALT WAS WORKED

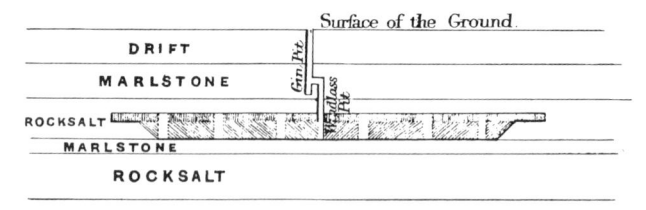

METHOD BY WHICH THE BOTTOM BED OF ROCK SALT IS NOW BEING WORKED

PLAN OF MARSTON HALL ROCK SALT MINE.

Scale, 4 Chains to an Inch.

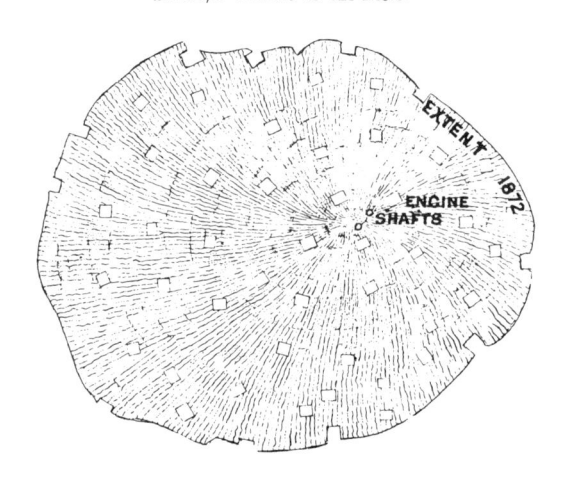

SECTION.

LEFT: These drawings illustrate methods of working mines in 1882. RIGHT: Victorian mine displays the huge pillars left to support the rock above. (ICI) BELOW: Working men in caps, foreman in a bowler; shoes and ties show this is a visit, not work. (ICI)

86

ABOVE: The Marston Mine, 1896. Ponies grew too big to return to the surface; glossy coats resulted from licking rock-salt. (ICI) BELOW: Salt arch erected for the opening of the Verdin Technical Schools in 1897. (NC)

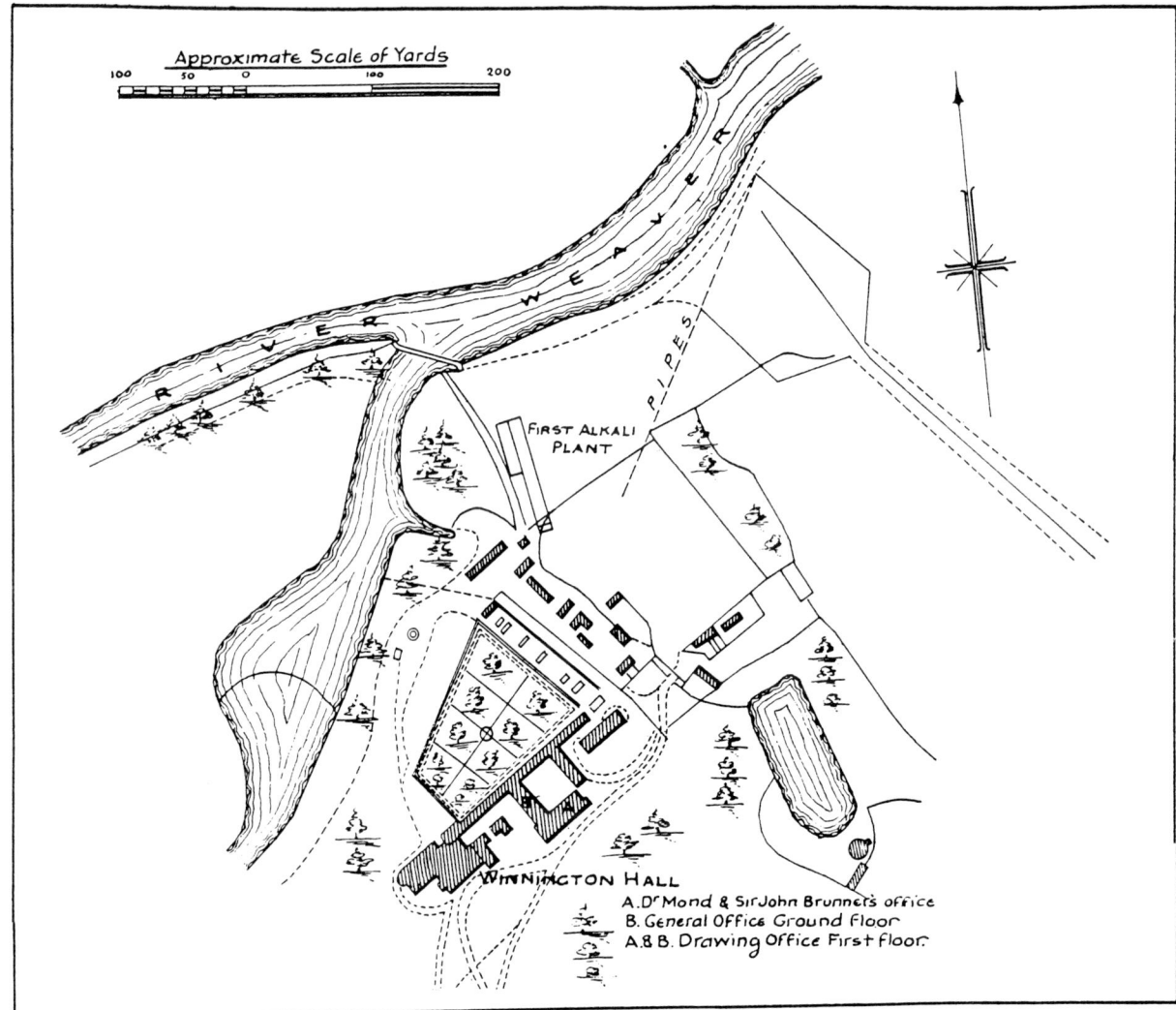

ABOVE: 'The Partners', taken in stereoscope for the Brunner Mond Silver Jubilee. (MH) BELOW: Plan of the first works, built in 1874. (ICI)

88

Pioneering Partners: Brunner Mond

The story of the chemical industry of Mid-Cheshire is tinted with romance. It was founded in 1862 by two remarkable men. John Tomlinson Brunner was the son of a Swiss immigrant school-master from Liverpool. His knowledge of business allowed him to rise to become the chief clerk at the soda ash works of John Hutchinson & Co at Widnes.

There he met the young Ludwig Mond. From an orthodox German Jewish background, Mond had been a student of Professor Bunsen in Heidelberg. He did not complete his degree because he was called to do military service. His parents paid for a substitute to go in his place because of anti-semitism, thus spending the money saved to keep him at University. They encouraged him to settle in England where the political success of Disraeli suggested discrimination was less institutionalised. The dearth of trained English scientists at the time allowed easy access for immigrants into industrial positions. The two young, intelligent men became close friends.

Mond was employed to try to solve the major problem of soda manufacture. A side-product of the Le Blanc process, then in use, was a black sulphorous sludge which was dumped in vast piles. Along with acid fumes from the factories, the effects on the surroundings were devastating; hardly a blade of grass survived and Widnes smelled strongly of bad eggs.

Soda ash was originally made by burning sea-weed to extract the soda, hence 'ash'. It was an essential ingredient of soap and is used to produce clear glass but is used by hundreds of other industries.

Mond became aware of the developments in soda ash production made by Ernest Solvay in Belgium. He agreed with Brunner to set up their own works and signed a licence from Solvay on 23 September 1872. The essential ingredients of Solvay's process were brine and limestone. On 4 May 1873 the partners travelled to Hartford Station and walked along the Weaver Valley to Winsford looking for a site to pump brine. Local land-owners did not want a Widnes-type factory close to their homes and would not sell.

Eventually Edward Milner, owner of salt-works at Anderton, suggested that the Winnington Hall Estate of Lord Stanley might be suitable. Milner showed it to them from his works overlooking the valley. There was a good river frontage for export of finished goods and a plentiful supply of brine. A branch line existed from the Cheshire Lines Railway for the delivery of limestone from Buxton. Mond declared 'That is the spot', but doubted they could afford it.

Brunner's commercial skill arranged loans and mortgages through Parr's Bank (by the Dane Bridge) and from others they raised the capital.

At first they intended to demolish the old hall but, as they needed somewhere to live, the two wings became separate homes. The stables served as offices, the hayloft as a drawing office and a wooden shippon housed the smithy and laboratory.

As they were about to move in Salome Brunner died only a week after giving birth to their sixth child. Jane Wyman, the daughter of a doctor, was engaged as a housekeeper/governess and within 18 months married Brunner. Frida Mond never accepted this and always considered her as little better than a servant. At the Company Silver Jubilee Lady Brunner gained the upper hand in the feud which developed between the women. Neither wanted to sit on the same platform as the other. Lady Brunner sent a message to say she could not attend 'as she has been commanded by the Queen to attend at her drawing room'. Victoria was less concerned with social background than Frida Mond.

Mond had a bed prepared in the works to be on hand in case of problems and had a bell hung outside his bedroom so that he could be called to sort out any emergency. Both partners worked three nights a week, ensuring constant supervision during working hours. Mond recorded 'everything that could break down did break down and everything that could burst did burst'. The first day's production was wrecked when Solvay, helping on the auspicious occasion, accidentally turned off a safety valve. In 1874, 838 tons of soda were made at a loss of £4,300. In 1875, 2,408 tons were produced and a profit of £2,405 was recorded. The next year Mond commented 'We are not making chemicals, we are making money!'. Ten years later Brunner could afford to leave the company to managers and to follow a political career.

The process developed by Solvay separates the molecules of the two raw materials. The sodium and chloride of salt and the calcium and carbon of limestone rebind in ammonia as sodium carbonate (soda ash) and calcium chloride. The latter is discharged as waste.

In 1897 soda ash works at Lostock were built by Messrs Bowman Thompson & Co, making use of the Holford Brine Field, where the first 1,000 feet of earth contained 600 feet of solid rock salt. Lostock was taken over by Brunner Mond in 1910. It used a slightly different process than Winnington and added sulphuric acid and bleaching powder to the company products.

Mond was one of the most respected scientists of his day. He was President of the Society of Chemical Industry in 1889 and elected Fellow of the Royal Society in 1891. In 1892 he received an honorary LlD from Padua University and was known as 'The Doctor' from then on, affording him great pride as he had been unable to graduate. Brunner received an honorary doctorate from Liverpool University and was its Pro-Vice Chancellor.

In 1881 Brunner Mond became a public limited company and the partners sold their interests to the new company. Both were made joint Managing Directors for life. Joseph Crossfield, the soap manufacturer of Warrington, one of their chief customers, was the first chairman. The new company had a nominal capital of £600,000 divided into £10 shares.

The Brunners and Monds spent more time away from Winnington and the Hall evolved into a Social Club in 1899. The company recruited from Oxbridge, and with its centre at the Hall Club, a college-like community developed at Winnington. This community spirit was strengthed because managers had to live less than 10 minutes away from their work-place to be summoned in emergency. Many lived in Greenbank and Hartford. The elegant rooms at Winnington were used for social functions, musical evenings, lectures and theatricals. Catering was of the best and the cellars contained rare vintages. Rooms were available for visiting managers. A golf course existed near Moss Road where the names 'Golf' or 'The Links' are still used. The golf moved to Sandiway when land was purchased from Lord Delamere around Pettypool for shooting and fishing parties.

During the First World War Brunner Mond supported the war effort. With men in the sevices women were recruited to work in most departments. At the outbreak of war supplies of explosives were not sufficient. The Company's knowledge of ammonia production devised completely new methods to produce nitrate of ammonia, used in the production of TNT.

Before the war only 1,000 tons a year were produced by the whole country. By 1918 it had risen to 85,000 tons. Much research was conducted by Dr Francis Freath, who was honoured with an OBE for his services.

On the day after the Armistice Freath asked Lord Moulton to send him and colleagues to Germany 'to pinch everything [scientific developments] they've got'. Moulton had been appointed to improve the British chemical industry in the war and agreed. Freath made for the BASF plant at Oppau which worked on nitrates, successfully extracting them from the atmosphere. The management would not allow them to measure or draw anything but Freath reconstructed what he had seen from memory. War-time research in Northwich and what was taken from Germany made modern intensive farming possible, using artificial fertilizers based on nitrates.

Albert Tangye worked out a way of producing synthetic phenol for the explosives industry at Lostock in a laboratory nicknamed 'The Devil's Kitchen. After a disastrous explosion in 1917 at Silvertown near London, work on TNT moved to an open-field site at Gadbrook without risk to civilian lives and property. A serious fire broke out and two managers played hoses on the machinery until it burnt out, preventing another disaster. After the war the works became Broadhurst's Garden Bakeries, providing work for the wives and daughters of ICI men living on Rudheath Estate.

From the 1860s Winnington became the company village and this all but merged with Barnton. Management settled in Hartford. With the take-over of the works at Lostock, Northwich became almost a company town. From 1862 hardly any aspect of Northwich life could escape the influence of the Brunner Mond works. Mond lived a quiet, secluded intellectual life but Brunner threw himself into every aspect of local life.

Brunner's granddaughter, Shelagh Salome Brunner, married Prince Ferdinand Andreas de Lichtenstein on 14 January 1925. A special Act had to be passed by the state's Parliament to allow him to marry a commoner. On 8 June 1961 Brunner's great granddaughter, Katherine Lucy Mary Worsley, married the Duke of Kent in York Minster. She was the guest of honour when Winnington works celebrated its centenary, an ironic sequel to the Silver Jubilee.

A further Royal association with the area was that Group Captain Peter Townsend, who some expected to marry Princess Margaret in the 1950s, was the grandson of Northwich solicitor, George Hatt Cooke. He was born in India but spent part of his childhood at his grandfather's home at Hartford Hall, where his Indian nurse attracted much curiosity.

Lostock works with Cheshire Lines rail wagons, used to bring limestone from Derbyshire. (ICI)

Winnington 1974: beyond the works is the factory village. (AH)

White Slaves and Other Workers

The antiquity of salt making was responsible for particular working conditions which, by the 19th century, caused great concern. It was morality that was foremost in reformers' minds, before risks to health, life and limb, effects on family life or the welfare of children.

From the earliest times the family was an economic unit. Wives and children were expected to help husbands. This was obvious in a pre-industrial agricultural economy, where children helped gathering crops and in the home. In the salt towns industrial work took over from agriculture. In the Middle Ages the work of drawing salt from the pans was undertaken by women.

This tradition continued until the 19th century, although the salt pans were far too big to be worked by women. Men stoked fires and drew salt, but women and children helped them. Women loaded, moved and bagged salt besides preparing food and drink. The salt proprietor provided pans with a supply of coal and brine, then purchased the finished salt at a fixed price. It was up to the labourer to produce as much as was humanly possible for the least cost. Large families were favoured as more hands within the family produced more salt.

Before women and children were excluded from the salt-pans by the Factory Act of 1876 at least 40% of those employed were women and children. A family with 43 members working in the same works as a sort of co-operative was recorded.

Because of the heat men worked without shirts in flannel knee-length breeches and women in undergarments, which hung closely because of perspiration. It was this near nudity which aroused Victorian ire, although steam around the pans was so dense that no-one could see another person unless close enough to touch. The reputation for loose morals and scanty clothes attracted visitors with voyeuristic rather than scientific curiosity.

Families hardly left their place of work during the week; meals were heated by lowering containers into the hot brine. The whole family slept where they could find warmth, either in the hot-house or in the stoking area, where there was risk from fire or scalding. Mothers breast-fed babies by the pans and the baby would sleep in a fuel basket. This was acceptable — by contemporary standards — within the same family, but not when several families were involved.

Even worse to Victorian moralists, vagrants sheltered for the night in the warm, dry work-place in exchange for helping with the work. One such was 'Poor Old Mick' (Michael Gray) who was found dying of exposure on the Weaver tow-path in January 1875. He had no home, earning a meagre living doing odd jobs sleeping in out-buildings or salt works. The factory inspector's report that year mentions frequent complaints about such people using the salt works. It was more concerned that they damaged salt by sleeping on it than the need for reform. Vagrants prefered to put up with such conditons than enter the Workhouse.

Small children helped to break lumps with hammers before it was bagged. As sons became old enough they hired themselves as labourers with years of practical experience. This piece-work arrangement ensured that there was little opportunity for time-off, much less holidays.

It was possible for hard-working families to save enough to purchase their own pans, becoming self sufficient. After women and children were excluded from working by the pans the labourers requested a rise to compensate for lost income. When it was not forthcoming they went on strike. Herman Falk, of Winsford, blamed other salt works for giving the rise because the owners were mainly 'Men who had risen from the ranks themselves' and had great sympathy for the labourers.

Frida Mond, Ludwig's wife, would not mix socially with salt proprietors as they were working men who had risen by the efforts of their own hard work. When Hartford Church opened one lady objected to sitting 'between a salt maker and a soap boiler'. They were Sir Jospeh Crossfield and Sir Joseph Verdin, whose wealth and titles came from the 'trade'. Colonel Marshall, the last of the family to be involved with salt, objected to even being listed as such, preferring his military titles.

The fires were extinguished on Friday to cool the pans. This gave workers the Sabbath for relaxation and worship. On Monday the scale which formed at the bottom of the pans was removed before boiling started. This gave women the only opportunity to hang washing out before the air became soot-laden again.

Workers started at 2 or 3 am and could work until 10 or 11 pm, snatching what little sleep they could. Safety aspects were non-existent. Men sometimes fell into boiling brine and were scalded to death. It was not until the 1920s that an overhead hand-rail, which they could try to catch hold of if they slipped, became standard. Sometimes they fell because they were so tired. Boiling brine could splash over the stokers until a protective shield known as a 'caboodle' was introduced above their heads.

Coarse salt was made by slow simmering, often for several weeks. Gangs of four labourers were hired for a couple of days to 'draw' the crystals from the pans at the end of this time. They had no job security.

Danger was ever-present, loading coarse salt along short piers jutting from the buildings overhanging the waterfront. In icy or wet weather clogs slipped, sending men tumbling forwards. With luck they landed on the soft salt; often they fell on hard wood or metal to be injured or killed.

Conditions on the boats were as bad, particularly in winter. It was possible, by using the family, to save enough money (around £800 in 1840) to purchase their own vessel. The Weaver Flats were a special boat of 80-100 tons developed for the salt trade. They were called flats because of their wide, flat bottoms for piling salt or coal for easy unloading with a shovel. One horse or between four to six men pulled them. By working as a family the cost (5s per man for a trip to Liverpool in the 1840s) was saved. Without the family to help, men would have to be paid to load and unload them too.

Vessels were not allowed to move on the river on Sundays. On Saturday nights the men came ashore; after cleaning the vessels they put on their best boatman's costume, spending the evening and night ashore. Near the river there were numerous pubs which attracted women, including prostitutes, to help them spend.

The families who worked to purchase the flats became some of the most respected workers, living in a separate community in Navigation Road. Developed around 1860, the houses had fanlights above and pilasters flanking the doors, among the finest workers' houses in the town.

In the early years of Brunner Mond conditions were poor. The most objectionable aspect was the two-shift system, used throughout the chemical industry, by which the works ran non-stop. Even if the shift allowed workers to be at home on a Sunday they were asleep for most of the day.

At Winnington work conditions were often dreadful and the worst area was the Milky Lime Department. The socialist leader, Tom Mann, took a job there. He had organised the London Dockers' Strike of 1889 which was the first successful strike by unskilled workers. Mann became self-appointed champion of the unskilled and the conditions at Winnington were taken up by Keir Hardie, the first Labour MP, who published accounts in the socialist press. Few men, they wrote, were able to stand the pace. The work was described as 'horses work'. All day, men wheeled cast-iron barrows of hot milky lime from the furnace up a plank walk to tip it into a tank. No break was allowed in a shift lasting twelve hours; food and drink were taken on the move. The fumes from the lime made men sick, worsened by lack of nourishment. Some men could not last a full day and few managed to last for a couple of months. Local men refused to work there and many Irish labourers were imported.

The lime kilns needed continual loading. Great numbers of men carried baskets of coke or lime which were tipped in at the top where the fumes, smoke and heat belched out. Many were badly burned and were described as 'poor specimens of humanity' after a year's work. The grinding mills were 'like being in a snuff box'. Slowly conditions improved by mechanisation and research.

The conditions, houses linked to jobs and the lack of union activity caused the workers to be nicknamed 'The White Slaves of Winnington'. It is sometimes implied that Brunner and Mond objected to unions. On the contrary, Brunner addressed meetings urging salt-workers to join a trade union when the Salt Union was formed in 1888, as he could foresee the problems to come. He provided Guildhalls at Winsford and Runcorn for union meetings to be held away from factories to prevent intimidation.

The Winnington men were not concerned to join a union as they were, presumably, content with pay and conditions. During a dispute in Widnes chemical works in 1889, a group of pickets from there threatened to prevent goods entering or leaving Winnington. Brunner stood on a barrel in the yard beggings an emergency meeting to join the Union so that they could all get back to work. Mann's writings must be understood as those of a socialist activist trying to discredit a prominent Liberal MP. Brunner and Mond themselves worked alternately on the same 84 hour shifts at first. Eventually working hours were reduced, canteen and social facilities were provided. A week's holiday with pay was also provided from 1884. A sick club operated from the start; in 1902, following legislation, the Company took full responsibility. Brunner Mond became one of the most enlightened employers in the country. Work hours were cut from 12 hours a day to eight, but with a 10% reduction in pay in 1889. This was again reduced to a 47 hour week of eight hours a day and Saturday morning in 1919 and a five day week in 1947.

The Times called Brunner a 'Chemical Croesus' after the fabulously rich monarch of Greek legend. When Lady Brook criticised his election victory he claimed he had 'filled more hungry stomachs and founded more happy homes than all the Brookes and all the Mainwarings'. Few could disagree.

In 1928 the Warrington Bakers, Broadhurst & Co, moved to the former munitions factory at Gadbrook to open their Garden Bakeries. Associated with the development of Rudheath as a garden suburb, the two factories, one for cakes, the other for biscuits, provided 500 jobs by 1939 on a 23-acre site. Surrounded by attractive gardens, the bakery provided excellent canteen facilities. This doubled as a social club and could be hired for parties and wedding receptions. The grounds included sports fields and tennis courts while the company employed a registered nurse in its surgery. The Garden Bakeries were developed to provide employment for wives and daughters of workers at Lostock as pioneers of modern factory conditions, but were closed after take-overs despite great worker loyalty.

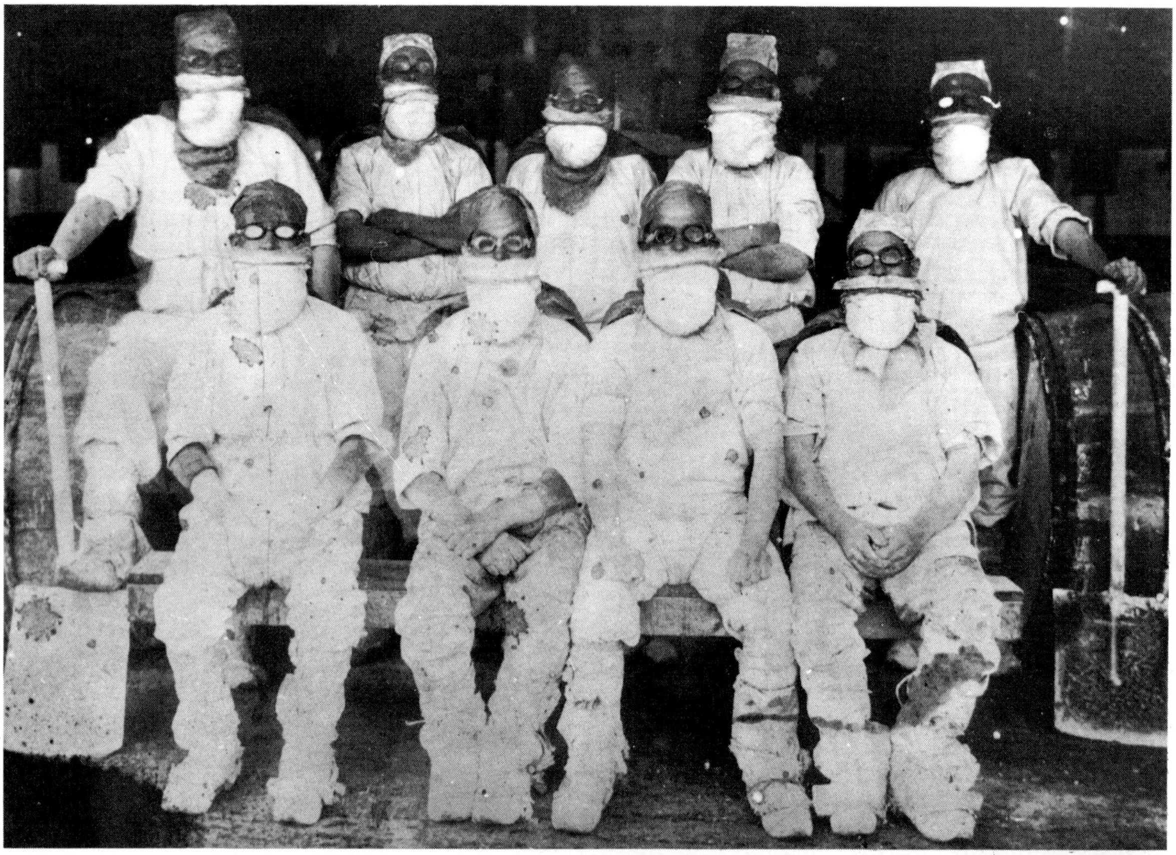

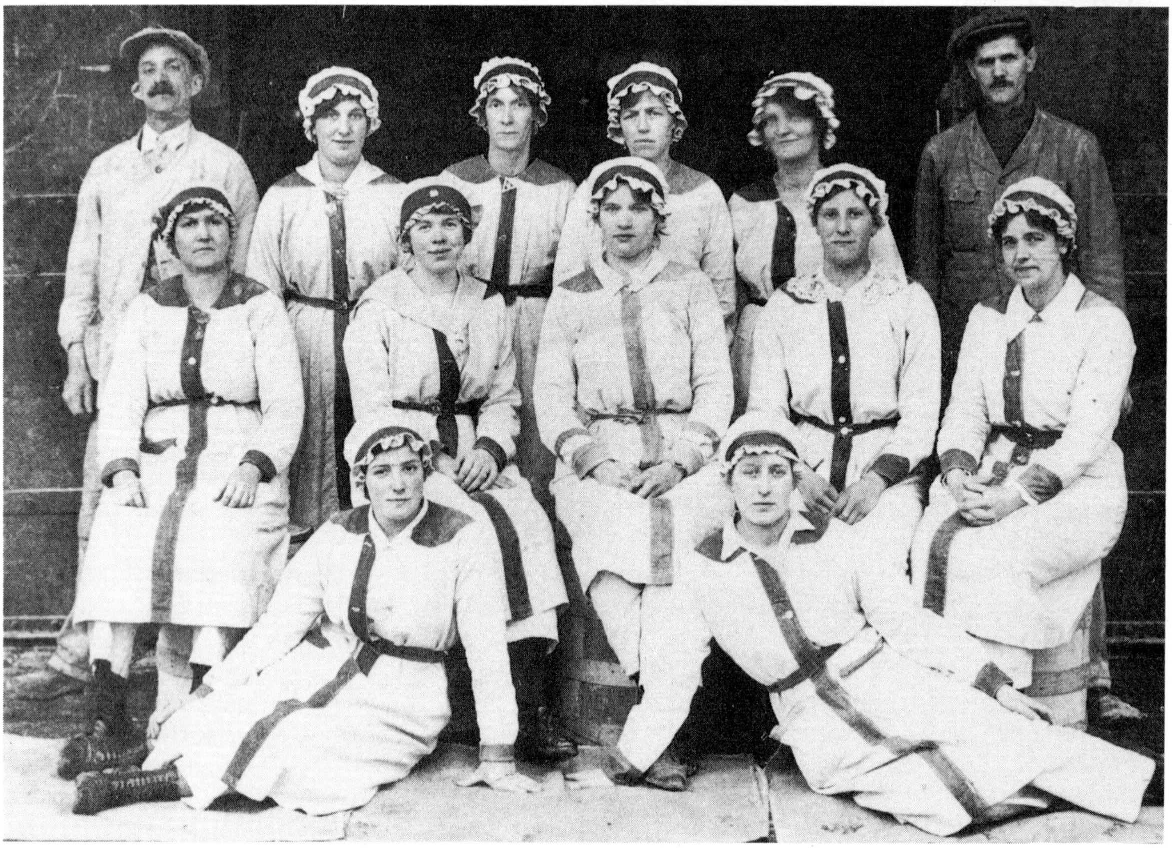

OPPOSITE ABOVE: Smile! Bleach packers in 1917. (ICI) BELOW: Women workers during World War I; protective clothing included trousers for modesty. ABOVE: Testing American protective clothing, evidently for lab workers before World War I. (ICI) BELOW: Improved bleach packing between the wars. (ICI)

ABOVE: Broadhurst's stark Modernist cake factory in 1949. (BB). CENTRE: The famous gardens outside the canteen and bungalow-like office. (BB) BELOW: Untouched by human hand: cake production in 1949. (BB)

ABOVE: Biscuit-making used conveyor-belt production lines. (BB)
BELOW: Teenagers and grandmothers are hardly distinguishable in this 1940s photo in Broadhurst's canteen. (BB)

STONING THE POLICE ON ELECTION DAY.

At the Northwich Petty Sessions on Monday the magistrates had before them a case in which a labourer named Emmanuel Hankey, residing in York-buildings, was charged with assaulting P.C. Samuel Ford, stationed at Macclesfield.—Mr. J. H. Cooke prosecuted, and Mr. J. J. Dixon defended.—The statement of Mr. Cooke, and the evidence of P.S. Handford and P.C. Ford, was to the effect that about eight o'clock on the night of the election day, after the Riot Act had been read, while the police were blocking up two ends of High street and also one end of Market-street, the defendant was seen by Handford to stoop down and pick up something, which he threw among the officers. Hankey then got round some women, and went off down the street. The missile thrown by the defendant struck Ford on a button on the chest with sufficient

ABOVE: Police during the 1892 strike. (CJL) BELOW: The opening of the Verdin Technical School in 1897 by the Duchess of Westminster. INSET: Report of disturbance during the 1895 election. (NC)

100

Repaying the Community

Queen Victoria's Golden and Diamond Jubilees (1887 and '97) gave the impetus for gifts which perpetuate the names of Verdin and Brunner locally. These were a way in which the families repaid the community from which they derived their wealth. The two families contested local elections but the gifts were genuine gifts of philanthropy, not election bribes.

The 1885 election was the first where all men over 21 could vote and the first by secret ballot. New constituencies were created, including Northwich, covering Winsford, Middlewich and Runcorn. John Brunner stood against Robert Verdin 'The Salt King', to be the first Liberal candidate at a meeting in the Drill Hall on 11 April.

The Liberals, standing for reform, were expected to win Northwich. Brunner pledged himself to policies which he held throughout his life. He is best remembered for gaining compensation for those suffering the effects of salt subsidence and for championing Irish Home Rule. He wanted schools free from religious denominations and to end the Anglican position as the Established Church, with Bishops in the House of Lords. He objected to the hereditary Lords.

Verdin expressed approval of elementary education but objected to providing further funding as, like subsidence compensation, it would increase the rates. The meeting elected Brunner, whom Verdin accused of filling the hall with his supporters, refusing to congratulate him.

Instead he took his support to the Conservatives, ensuring that his younger brother, William Henry, was elected as their candidate. Verdin's campaign speeches criticised Brunner for his religious views, questioning his patriotism (because of his Swiss father and Jewish/German partner). He criticised work conditions, using the term 'White Slaves of Winnington' for the workers. This backfired when it was revealed that the Verdins were Brunner Mond shareholders.

Brunner was elected on 1 December, after serious disruptions. The town was packed with voters from outlying areas. Those from Winsford travelled in flats. At dusk unease was felt and traders shuttered windows. Those at the Conservative offices were smashed and the Riot Act was read. Violence came from both sides. The police charged with truncheons in the narrow winding streets, creating panic.

Brunner appointed Thomas Edward Ellis, a Welsh Oxford graduate, as his election secretary, later financing his Parliamentary career. Gladstone's government collapsed over the issue of Irish Home Rule and in 1886 Brunner faced a second general election. The electorate lost confidence in Gladstone. Brunner was ill during the crucial weekend before the election and victory went to Robert Verdin, standing as a Liberal Unionist. This faction kept Liberal ideals but wanted Ireland to be ruled from London and was allied to the Conservatives. *The Times* enthused about 'the greatest Liberal Unionist victory in the Country'.

Brunner left for a world tour, which he described in articles in the *Chronicle*. He visited Egypt, later endowing the chair of Egyptology (and two others) at Liverpool University.

Verdin proved a disappointing MP, only attending the House to argue for English landowners in Home Rule debates, as the Verdins held Irish estates. This offended the many Irish workers in Mid-Cheshire. Brunner returned on 2 July 1887 and 'the entire population of the district' turned out to cheer. Two steamboats loaded with people and a brass band came from Winsford. The streets were decorated and at Solvay Road the horses were taken from his carriage and ecstatic workmen pulled it to Winnington Hall.

Just three weeks later Verdin died from a heart attack and a by-election was called. Irish Home Rule was the main issue. Lord Henry Grosvenor, third son of the Duke of Westminster, stood as a Unionist. Attention from the whole country, Ireland and Irish Americans focussed on Northwich. Brunner's victory was celebrated in Dublin and New York, convinced that Home Rule was assured.

Brunner held the seat safely until he retired in 1906. By then the Liberals were giving way to the Labour Party and, before he died, Brunner spoke and voted for Labour candidates. His eldest son, John, represented Northwich until 1918 and his grandson contested the seat in 1945.

It was only after much soul-searching that, in 1894, he accepted a Baronetcy, allowing him to keep his seat in the Commons but to use and pass on a title. He believed it would give him greater influence in his public work. After retiring he was offered a seat in the Lords. He considered becoming Lord Everton (after his birthplace) but decided against betraying his principals.

The Verdins started as boat owners on the Weaver in the 1840s. Joseph Verdin (1807-1873) founded the family fortune with salt works in Northwich, Middlewich and Winsford. Of five sons from his second marriage only William Henry, the youngest, married and was Sheriff of Cheshire during the 1897 Jubilee year.

Mond donated generously to many public institutions with gifts to support subscriptions. He is remembered for the Davey Faraday Research Laboratories which he presented to the Royal Society. His bequest of 56 Rennaissance masterpieces to the National Gallery with an extension to house them was the most valuable gift of art given to the nation. They form the core of the display in the Sainsbury Wing.

Moves to set up a public library in Northwich failed in 1883, because the Local Board would not increase the rates to pay for it. Brunner gave land in Witton Street, demolishing three shops to build the library which opened on 21 July 1885 amid great rejoicing. He gave many books and encouraged others to donate used books. Brunner was a pioneering figure in providing libraries. The Libraries and Museums Act of 1850 hindered the opening of both by insisting on free services but that two thirds of the rate-payers had to agree to the expense. The Brunner Library was one of the first administered by a Local Board, containing a museum and art display.

The Library was damaged by subsidence and a new building was provided in 1909. A doctor's surgery and a solicitor's office flanked the entrance; their rents helped cover library costs. Upstairs a flat reduced costs as the librarian accepted a lower salary with free accommodation.

His daughters operated a lending service for employees from his Library at Winnington Hall. This prompted him to set up a reading room and library in the works. When the Northwich Library opened the Council took responsibility, making it the first local authority library in any village.

In 1886 Brunner helped pay for the erection of the Gladstone Liberal Club on land next to the Library. Until it was destroyed by fire in 1977 it had a balcony at the front from which candidates addressed meetings and Brunner's election victories were announced. The Conservative Club was built in 1913 with a similar balcony.

The British Association visited Northwich four times in Victoria's reign. The 1887 visit gave Mond the idea of a Salt Museum. Brunner provided a building behind the Library. It was a pioneering venture containing study facilities with books on salt, graphs, diagrams, maps and photographs. It was probably the first industrial museum and certainly the first museum dedicated to a single product.

Its early promise was lost when the Honorary Curator, Thomas Ward died. He was a Director of the Salt Union and expert on the industry, having visited many salt-producing areas as an agent for the Thompson family, who operated the Lion Salt works and had an office in Liverpool. No funding was ever provided and the building was requisitioned for Social Services in the First World War and demolished to construct Albion Way. The present Salt Museum houses some of the original exhibits.

Brunner gave the gold chain of office for the chairman of the Urban District Council to mark Victoria's Diamond Jubilee.

Robert Verdin gave the infirmary, the park named after him and the baths which were once in it for the Golden Jubilee. A timber-framed structure covered a large iron-lined pool and individual baths, attracting people with illnesses which were eased by swimming in brine. They became something of a health spa and were surrounded by bowling greens and recreation facilities aimed at improving health. Earlier baths were opened in 1840 by Dr James Dean specifically for medical use. The park was formerly the grounds of Winnington Bank House, which Verdin converted and donated to the town as the Victoria Infirmary, marking the Golden Jubilee. The park, baths and infirmary were all linked to providing health care.

It was ironic that, following Verdin's objections to subsidence compensation, the baths were destroyed by subsidence, bringing down his statue.

Sir Joseph Verdin provided magnificent terra-cotta fronted Technical Schools as an 1897 Jubilee gift when Northwich was richly decorated for the opening. He established a fund from his own money to compensate for hardship caused by subsidence in 1891. When Parliament passed the Brine Compensation Bill the fund became redundant and was changed to provide scholarships for poor students to attend the schools.

Sir Joseph lived at Brockhurst, providing timbered houses for his estate workers on London Road. Among his guests was the Prince of Wales (later Edward VII), who presented a mosaic floor to commemorate his visit. Queen Victoria controlled the Prince's income to curb his wild ways but he found wealthy men like Verdin only too willing to provide lavish hospitality.

The Prince often visited the Earl of Enniskillin at Hartford Grange. As Lord Cole, before becoming Earl, he and the Prince were implicated in a divorce case when a subpeona was served on the heir to the throne in 1871. The court disregarded the evidence, claiming the lady was 'deranged'. The Earl was Master of the Cheshire Hounds and the Prince pursued foxes by day and clandestine romances at night. On one visit he arrived by an earlier train than expected and walked from Hartford Station to the Grange without anyone taking any notice.

The Earl's daughter married the third Baron Delamere of Vale Royal. They, with her brothers and the sons of Cecil de Trafford of Hartford Manor, became leaders of the fun-loving community in Kenya's Happy Valley. They are central figures in the book *White Mischief*.

The 1880s and 1890s were times of elaborate celebrations. Besides the Jubilees, with their processions and parties, there were also parades for the opening of the various buidings and laying of foundation stones. There were victory celebrations after elections and the Boer War plus the Silver Jubilee of Brunner Mond. The streets were always lined with crowds and decorations abounded. Triumphal arches were erected. Most towns erected arches representing their major trades. Northwich had salt arches displaying the source of the town's prosperity. The Salt Union erected one with piers of 15 tons of cut rock salt with the arch of seven tons of blocks of white salt. A guard was posted to prevent the salt being stolen.

Other arches included barrels of chemicals from Brunner Mond, fire hoses from the fire-brigade and cycles from Isaac Robinson, the cycle manufacturer.

It was a philosophy of enlightened Victorian employers that, if men were given an extra few pence a week, they would squander it on drink. It was felt to be better to save all the pennies and after several years to give the people something 'worthwhile' (in their opinion) like a library or park.

Despite this generosity suspicions of loyalty were revived around the First World War. Mond's grandson stood for election at Chester and hecklers called out 'German'. When he explained that he was born in England and was English someone called out 'Yer a'nna, our cat's had kippers in a kipper box but they a'nna kippers!'.

Coachmen above the crowd which pulled Brunner's carriage to Winnington Hall in 1897. (ICI)

Proclaiming Edward VII in the Bull Ring, 1901 (ICI) and INSET: the same spot in the 1960s, with the carnival leaving High Street before pedestrianisation. (NC)

ABOVE: Salt arch erected for the opening of the Library in 1895. (NC)
BELOW: The 1988 Salt Arch used bagged salt as rock and block salt production had ceased. (DAN)

The Brine Zotofoam Baths are open for Ladies and Gentlemen daily.

mer Season, 9 a.m.—6 p.m.   Winter Season, 9 a.m.—5 p.m.

n Wednesday and Saturday these baths close at noon)

CHARGES

First Class (Non-Resident) 3/6   Six Tickets 18/-
         (Resident)   3/-   ,,   ,,   15/-
Second Class (Non-Resident) 2/-   ,,   ,,   10/-
         (Resident)   1/9   ,,   ,,   8/6

Brine used in the Zotofoam Baths at Northwich has been
ved by analysis to be the strongest obtainable and its efficacy
he treatment of rheumatism and kindred complaints has been
ved beyond doubt. It is advisable that Baths should be
viously booked.

H. CROSS.
Manager.

ABOVE: The Verdin Baths, Robert Verdin's monument and a cannon captured in the Crimean War. BELOW: From a 1950s brochure advertising the health advantages of the Brine Baths.

ABOVE: This land-slip made the baths unsafe. (NC) LEFT: Edward I, at the foundation of Vale Royal (1277): a glass panel, once at Vale Royal. RIGHT: The Earl of Enniskillin visited by Edward VII when he was Prince of Wales.

ABOVE: The Brockhurst was where Sir Joseph Verdin entertained the Prince of Wales. (NC) BELOW: The original Brunner Library and Gladstone Club. (NC)

ABOVE: The old Market Hall built in 1875. BELOW: The world's slowest 'mobile library' used to move half an inch a year. (NC)

110

DEMAND NOTE.

TOWNSHIP OF WITTON.

№ 660

Mr. *T. J. B. Hostage*

THE OVERSEERS of the Poor demand payment of the POOR and GAS RATES, made the Sixth day of December, 1848, due from you.

	£	s.	d.
Rateable Value	4	10	0
Amount of Rate at // in the Pound	0	4	6
Arrears			
Gas Rate at Six-pence in the Pound	0	2	3
	0	6	9

Feby 2d 49

Settled

SAMUEL HOLLAND, Assistant Overseer.

ABOVE: The Northwich Union Workhouse served as an old people's home until 1973. (NC) BELOW: Rate demand of 1849 to the Secretary of the Weaver Navigation. (CL)

111

LEFT: The diagram shows how pumping from flooded mines caused subsidence. RIGHT: The collapsed remains of the Witton Rock Salt Mine. BELOW: The canal was drained by subsidence at Marbury, 1907.
(NC)

One of England's Curiosities

A 19th century French writer advised tourists to visit Northwich to see buildings toppled in all directions, pools caused by collapsed mines and to visit the salt works and mines of what he called 'one of England's Curiosities'.

A description of 1898 said 'Northwich is the most crude and picturesque place it is possible for the mind to conceive. It is almost like what one could imagine a country place to be centuries ago'. It described homes like a shanty town lining narrow winding streets declaring 'every place has the appearance of foulness and decay'. The writer described buildings which leaned at all angles as if drunk and concluded Northwich had 'far too many pubs for its size and population'. Victorian middle and upper class people criticised drinking in pubs and beer-houses, believing it caused poverty and violence, but many of them drank just as much in their own homes.

Old photographs give the impression of an American gold rush town. Clothes and horse-drawn traffic are similar but the same method of building light-weight single or two-storey timber buildings were used. Victorian Northwich was like a gold-rush town with people coming to earn quick money in salt and other works before emigrating to the Wild West. It could have developed a prosperous air. However, many only wanted to spend the minimum for accommodation, so cramped lodging houses were the order of the day, while houses crumbled with the effects of subsidence. Shopkeepers had single storey timber-built shops in the town, but rather than live above them, they had brick suburban homes. It was unwise to build tall buildings; the Post Office is the only exception.

There were two types of subsidence. The first resulted from pumping 'wild brine' — natural underground streams which absorbed salt by running over salt beds. Rock salt is impervious but will dissolve. Where brine was pumped it was usually 'fully saturated' and could take up no more salt. However, where water seeped onto the rock salt it dissolved, often at a distance from the salt works. Eventually the ground above collapsed into the underground cavity and the hollow filled with water.

The second type occurred when mines were dug into the top bed of rock salt. The method was to dig bell pits where the shaft was sunk and miners dug out in all directions, creating a circular chamber. Often flooding occurred while the mine was in use. Miners heard the underground streams shortly before the water broke through. This was known as 'Roaring Meg' and was the sign to abandon the mine. The area north of the town was known as Dunkirk, as salt was exported into France *via* that port. Eventually it resembled the battlefield, covered with holes and pools created by collapsed mines.

Pit ponies went down as foals and grew too big to return to the surface in the coopered tubs which carried salt and men. When a mine was about to flood a slaughterer was called rather than let them drown.

At times subsidence was dramatic. Rushing air and water made pools around the subsidence bubble and boil or geysers of mud, brine and water squirted into the air while thunderings were heard in the depths of collapsing caverns.

Sometimes owners installed steam engines to pump water, which had absorbed salt and become brine, from flooded mines. This removed any support and the ground above, along with the pumping engine, collapsed.

One such occurred in 1838. 'A rock-house, tower, gin house, engine house, stables and two cottages were thrown into a heap of ruins at a depth of 15 yards from the surface; twelve individuals were also carried down and seven of them, overwhelmed by the falling ruin of the buildings, were taken out dead.'

An example of a flooded mine can be seen adjoining the Lion Salt Works. The Adelaide Mine was the last worked in the area and in the middle of the pool part of the mining equipment can just be seen showing above the surface.

Mining the bottom bed of rock salt, which was protected from seepage by the top bed, reduced the risk of collapse. Gradually controlled brine pumping in this bed was also introduced, using two pipes, one inside the other. Fresh water is pumped down the centre, forcing saturated brine up the outer pipe. Pumping continues until the chamber is the right size, then lime waste from chemical works is pumped down to fill the cavern, thus preventing subsidence.

Before this method for disposal of lime waste it was simply pumped into subsidence craters. The flat beds of lime between Witton and Marston were formed by filling the Ashton and Neumans Flashes, which were created by collapsed mines belonging to these families. A glance at the Ordnance Survey map gives the impression that Northwich is surrounded by large lakes. Unfortunately the demands of industry turned these pools into white wastelands.

One of the most interesting fillings was the Fury Pond on the opposite side of the Weaver from the town, which was caused by the collapse of Fury's Mine. A bank of cinders covered with clay and soil was constructed along the old line of the river, then lime waste was dumped in the lagoon behind it, forming a tree-covered hill 50 feet above water. The problem with this method is that it never completely sets and retains a blancmange-like texture, preventing use for building or almost any other purpose apart from land-fill rubbish tipping.

Rare lime-loving orchids flourish on these areas, descendants from seeds which travelled here on the wagons bringing limestone from Buxton to the chemical works.

The effects of wild brine pumping were unpredictable, with damage at a considerable distance from the works. It was impossible to prove whose works caused it.

The Cheshire Salt Districts Compensation Bill was progressed through Parliament by John Brunner. A select Committee under Sir Sidney Waterlow MP took evidence through March and April 1891. It levied a fixed rate of 3d on every 1,000 gallons of brine pumped, to establish a fund from which compensation was paid.

Brunner campaigned for this from his first election, introducing a Bill in 1891. Promoters were accused of simply wanting to stay at London's Grand Hotel. Opposition came from railway companies and the salt proprietors spent £5,000 to ensure it was defeated, because there was a depression in the trade and they could not afford to pay compensation.

Brunner was delighted when the Act was passed. He wrote 'I can honestly claim to have done more for my constituents than any Member of Parliament living or dead, for I have worked hard to obtain from Parliament an Act which involves me in a liability to pay from £800 to £1000 each year, and attaches that liability to my property for ever'. The Salt Union refused to pay until court action was threatened.

There were continual allegations from salt pumpers that subsidence around the confluence was caused by the dredging of the river. The Dane deposits vast quantities of sandy silt and a dredger is continually employed to clear it away. This, it was claimed, was the cause of sinking near the river.

The Subsidence Compensation Board, housed in a timber-framed building in Chesterway, conducted surveys to be sure that damage was actually caused by salt before payment was made. They could write off buildings, giving lump sums to those beyond repair. They also provided advice on building and gave grants to help build structures to resist subsidence.

The Cheshire prophet Robert Nixon once said that Northwich would be destroyed by water. In fact the old manor of Northwich has been totally destroyed and should be a lake.

Despite competitions to find a better solution to the problem the reintroduction of traditional timber-frame construction offered the best defence against damage. The timber held the brick infill (known as nogging) in place so that the buildings could withstand great movements, as when a building toppled backwards near to the gates of Verdin Park.

Buidings erected from the 1880s to the 1930s were mainly designed by the architects N. K. Ellerton, J. Crawley and A. W. Bostock and fall into three types. The first is a Victorian version of traditional Tudor timberwork, with solid frames using mortice and tenon joints held in place with projecting wooden dowels. They form impressive structures and imagination ran riot. They give a Victorian idea of Olde England influenced by the Vernacular Revival and the Arts and Crafts Movement. Decorations include cavaliers, cast-iron wyverns above the Bull Ring and a 1929 flapper over the former Northwich Building Society door.

Carved figures on Watling Street Chambers resemble ships' figureheads — sometimes included in buildings in ports. The idea might have been derived from Northwich's boatyards. Victorian machines copied repeating designs carved into timber. Plaster pargetting was used, some with Jacobean designs plus an appealing sheep and cow which were above a butchery. There are turrets and other features influenced by Romanticism.

An inferior use of timber was simply to use thinner lengths at intervals. The Revivalist buildings have timbers averaging eight to 10 inches. These functional buildings use timber strips around four to six inches, which are hardly jointed and infilled with brick. Both serve as a break to prevent cracks running along a wall.

The third group are the ones which make old photos look like the Wild West. The building method known as 'balloon framing' originated in Chicago and was used for boom towns in the USA. If the town failed, buildings could be taken to pieces and moved to the next town. No brick was used, with walls constructed of joists covered inside and out with planks. They were lightweight for easy movement or lifting in case of subsidence. They resemble the old West for they were often single-storeyed as the owner lived out of town away from smoke, flood or subsidence.

None of the three groups of structures was joined to their brick foundations. At various points there are areas, often of a slightly different brick, which could be removed. Jacks were inserted into each one and the building was raised on the solidly constructed timber base. Extra courses of bricks were added and the timber frame would be lowered again.

This can be seen at the Library, where a high brick foundation was provided as the building was moving at half an inch a year. This has ceased, but the high foundation allowed for plenty of sinking before jacking needed to take place.

Bridge House is now only part of a pub formerly standing by the Dane Bridge. As the building sank, water flowed into the cellar. In 1913 beer was served from barrels suspended above the bar until it too flooded. A new, lower building replaced it, which soon needed lifting. Then rollers from Yarwoods' boatyard were used to make a track, on which it was moved backwards and behind other buildings to be reset 185 feet away. This was not the end of its moves, for in 1955 a high brick foundation was built under it to raise it above the level of the 1946 flood waters. That flood was caused by unexpected rain. Sluice gates were opened on the Weaver downstream but those above the town could not be opened in time. Water backed up along the Dane, only to meet with the flash-flood from rain falling on hills above Congleton. Improved methods of weather forecasting and telephone communications between the sluice gate operators have all but eliminated the risk.

Buildings on either side of the Dane Bridge have high ground floors, keeping them above flood water. In 1955, after a risk of flooding, a meeting of tradesmen rejected plans to lift all the buildings in the town centre by up to five feet (the 1946 flood level). The increase of 3d on the rates was one reason but they believed the disturbance to buildings would cause people to shop elsewhere and numerous steps would exclude mothers with prams. The surface of High Street was raised by 20 feet in the first 20 years of this century. Liftable buildings were raised with it but brick buildings could not be.

Around the turn of the century Northwich was a town of steps; people either went up steps to buildings raised above flood level or went down steps to brick buildings which could not be raised.

The Crown Hotel has a cellar 30 feet below its present floor; the beer is stored in a room at ground level entered from the rear. The White Lion cellar is said to have been the ground floor rooms with the front door and windows blocked up in the walls. The Leicester Arms was the first pub to sink so deep that its parlour became a cellar. The Witch and Devil at Marston had a similar tale and was replaced by the New Inn when the landlord finally abandoned it to the advancing waters of the flash.

The internal walls of most buildings were covered with tongued and grooved planks, not plaster. This held brickwork in place, preventing falling plaster or bricks causing injury. Early examples are horizontal but later examples use diagonal boards for added resistance. In 1881 regulations prohibiting the erection of buildings without a frame were introduced in the town centre. This is noticeable at the Roebuck where the early 19th century front has a timber-framed extension at the rear.

Post-war buildings use a steel frame. They are also built in separate units, so that if one subsides it can be raised while the others can adjust. This can clearly be seen in the Shopping Centre where each unit has a small gap separating it from the next. In London Road the steel foundation rafts of post-war council houses can be seen.

Northwich's gas holder was of piston design, not the more usual expanding 'gasometer' type. This was necessary for added strength to contain gas in case of subsidence.

Central Northwich was made a conservation area in 1975. Since then many buildings in the area have vanished. Some were destroyed by arsonists, others by neglect or commercial pressures. Even where timber facades have been preserved there have been amusing results, as at Boots, where a prison-like extension was added and the decorative panels were replaced — upside down!

Flashes at Billinge Green away from salt works caused by pumping wild brine. (AH)

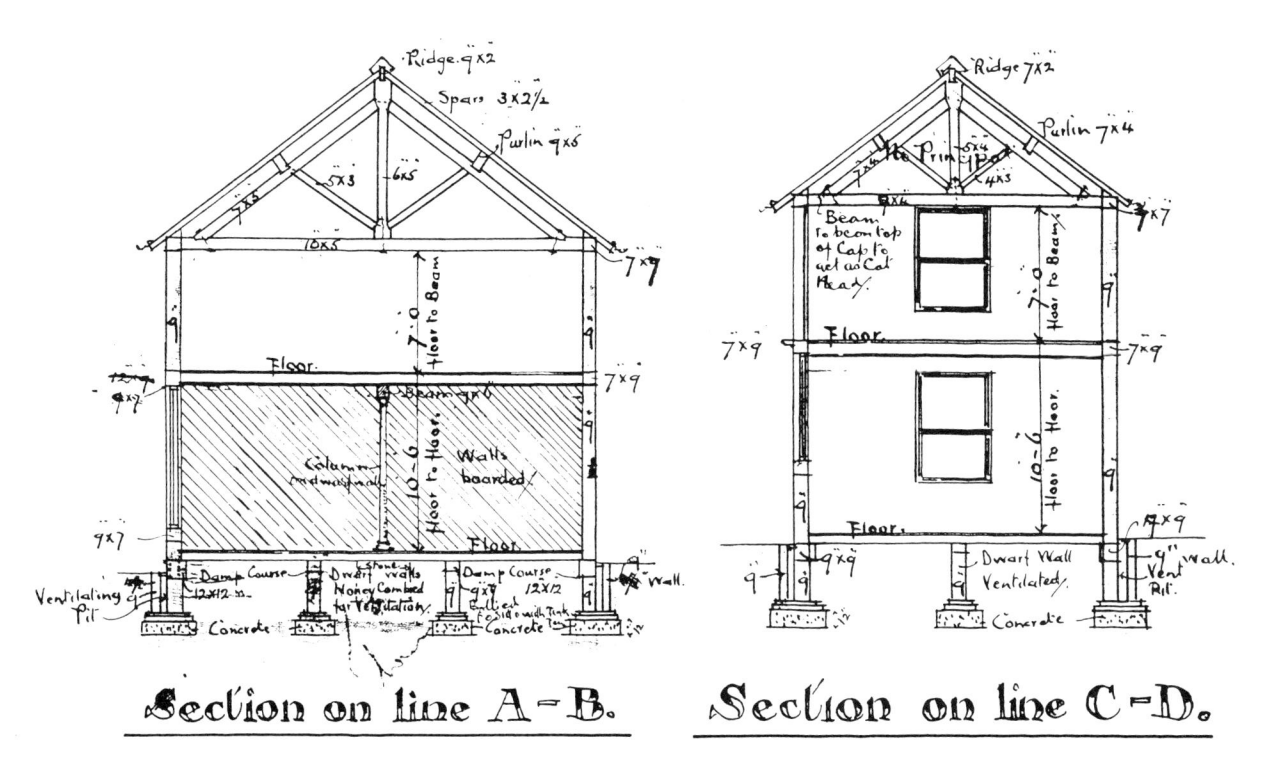

ABOVE: The road surface was destroyed by subsidence at Jubilee Street.
BELOW: The architect's drawing shows jacking points under buildings.
(BCB)

ABOVE: Streets were raised to keep them level so that brick buildings were partially buried. (NC) BELOW: Buildings did not fall into coveniently shaped holes! The streets were raised around them. (CL)

ABOVE: Windows and doors were mis-shapen by subsidence. (CL)
BELOW: Buildings were tilted out of true. (CL)

120

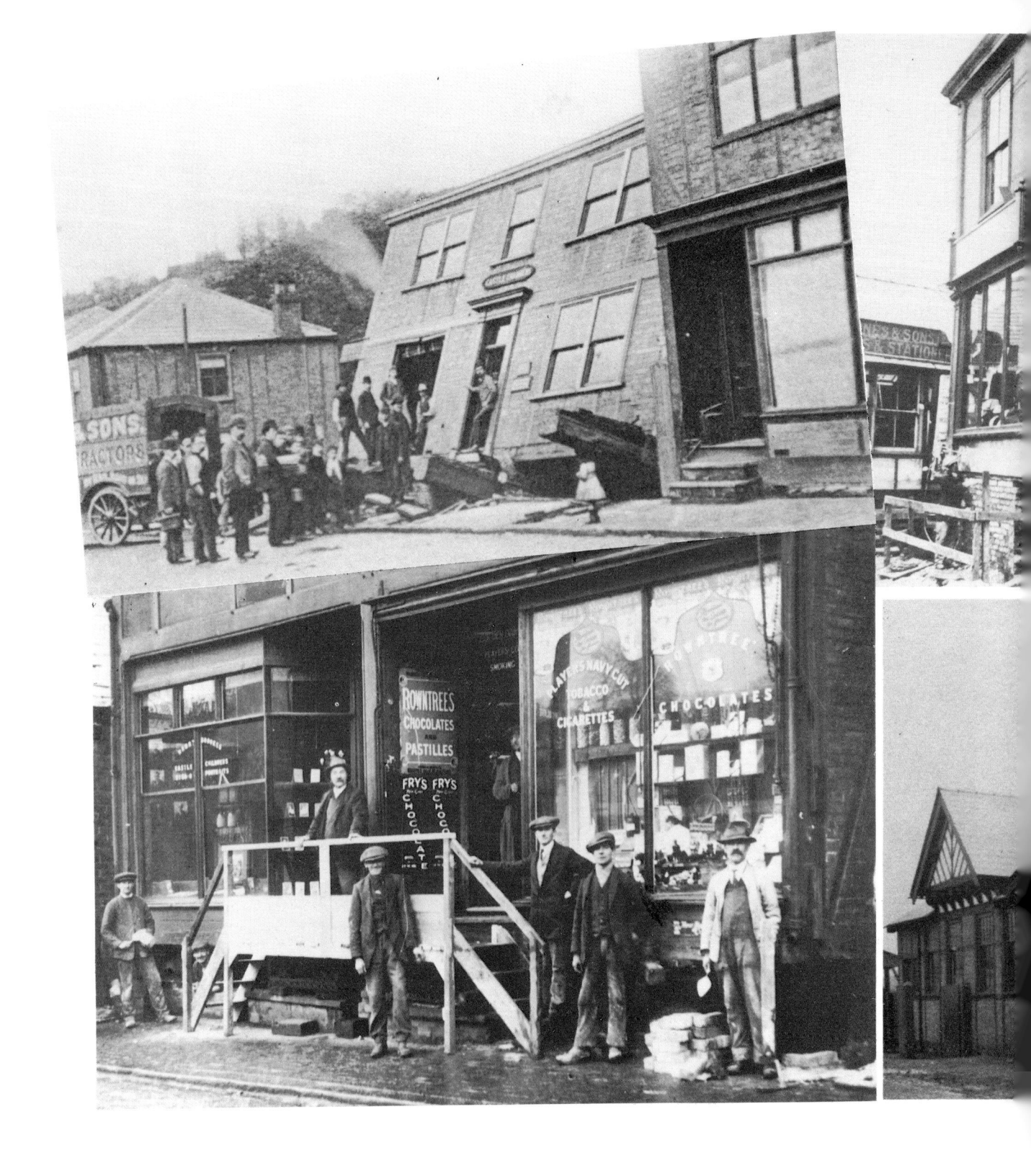

LEFT: Timber-framed buildings could withstand dramatic subsidences, as with Castle Chambers. (NC) BELOW: Shop-lifting was a necessity in Northwich! (CL) ABOVE: This example faced the Bullring and was raised to be above flood-water level. (NC) CENTRE: The timbered rear addition survived when the brick Wheatsheaf was destroyed and replaced in timber-frame. (NC) RIGHT: Preserving the top storey of a Vernacular Revival building above a new ground floor. (NC)

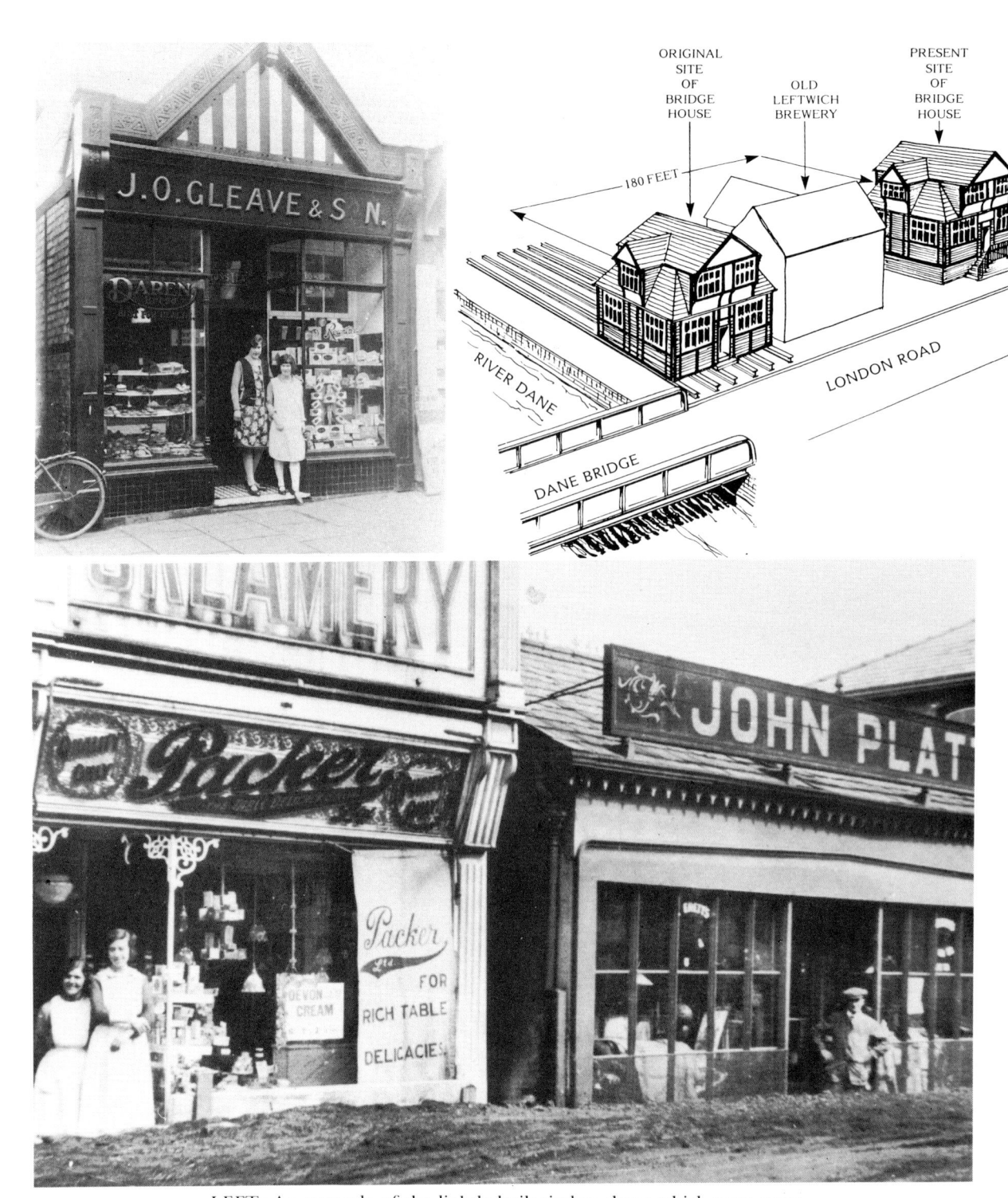

LEFT: An example of the lightly built timber shops which were once common. (NC) BELOW: The road had been raised but these buildings were suitable for lifting to the new level. (NC) RIGHT: This diagram shows how Bridge House made its 1913 move. (CAB)

LEFT: Raising the building on the original site. (NC) BELOW: Moving behind the Leftwich brewery. (NC) RIGHT: Lifted again in 1956 to the level of the adjoining garage above flood level. (NC)

ABOVE: Lagoons filled with lime waste at Wallerscote. (AH) CENTRE: Lostock Works and the lime beds. (AH) BELOW: It looks like Dodge City moved to Venice; balloon-framed single-storey shops in London Road, 1946. (NC)

The last major flood in 1946, with river-side buildings since demolished for rear access. (NC).

Birtles of Warrington were employed by Brunner to photograph results of subsidence as evidence to Parliament and record photos so that effects could be monitored; ABOVE: Three storey houses in Leicester Street had shutters to protect windows after dark, (CL) and BELOW: Crum Hill (here in 1891) was where the Market Hall is now and was occupied until 1963. (CL)

In Search of Paradise

Visitors to Victorian Northwich deplored the shanty-town appearance, overcrowding and filth. Yet much of that is now a conservation area! When the first houses on Rudheath estate opened in 1821 the Chairman of the Rural District Council described the new houses as a paradise and yearned for the day when Northwich was demolished.

From the early 18th century local brick became the usual building material. In the 19th century there were brickworks at Hartford and Lostock, the latter operated by Jabez Thompson, specialising in terra-cotta exterior decorations, as can be seen in Manchester Road and on the Technical School. Provision of brick housing developments for rent started in the 18th century with New Street (1775) and the Yorkshire Buildings (1780).

In 1802 Sir Thomas Bernard, a philanthropist involved in abolishing salt tax, came to Northwich from Oulton Park. He noticed 'At the entrance to the town . . . [London Road?] . . . rows of new houses built on each side of the way . . . and the neatness and elegance which these buildings give to the place'. He was told that they were not workers' houses but belonged to the 60 Revenue men who collected salt tax.

The rapid growth of the salt industry in the 19th century saw numerous terraced cottages built within walking distance of the works. It is difficult to determine exactly who built them. Some were provided by salt proprietors, but many of them had precious little capital and did not want to spend it.

Castle was a property of the Tollemache family who encouraged development of streets named after their estates at Peckforton and Beeston. Peckforton Castle was a result of their land management throughout Cheshire. This was the first extensive occupation of the hill since Roman times, consisting of small two-up, two-down cottages, of which Waterloo Terrace (1821) is s good example. Also in Waterloo Road, Twemlow Place was built by John Twemlow, a leading Methodist, to rent to members of the Church. He purchased cheap properties in the Witton sale to rent to Methodists.

The developments were planned schemes (more usually associated with housing built by factory owners) on a hill-top above and downwind of chimneys. Some houses had allotment-size gardens for growing food while provision of outside wash-houses and lavatories made them superior to much contemporary housing. Pleasant Street and Park Street, on Castle, Paradise Street near Witton Church and Golden Square at Hartford were named to sound attractive to potential buyers, indicating they were better-quality homes.

Some buildings were speculative. Rathbone Place on Castle was built as a pair by a builder and named after himself to rent to tenants. There were many examples of someone living in one house and charging rent to a few neighbours in property built for them. Others purchased neighbouring property as an investment and to control neighbours.

Sometimes a plot between two houses was built on, using existing walls, to build a dwelling needing only two walls and a roof, by people who could not afford the cost of four. At just 8½ bricks wide, 469 London Road, Davenham, is one such and is the smallest house in the area.

Housing which was adequate by the standards of the day could soon deteriorate because of lack of control or the greed of owners, as there was always a shortage. As one example, 26 and 28 Waterloo Road were small cottages with two rooms on each floor. The doors between front and back were blocked and they became true back-to-back houses with only one outside wall and door. Each single bedroom home housed over a dozen people. All the occupants of each cottage — more than 30 in each — shared a single undrained lavatory and tap.

Garrets and cellars were rented as separate dwellings. Without any regulation, occupants of overcrowded dwellings took in lodgers. There were always people looking for a place to sleep, particularly single men who came to work in the salt works to earn money to emigrate.

Much of what is now the market and shopping area was covered with cheap lodging houses. There people shared rooms and even beds; either several to a bed or the night shift following the day shift. Ford's Model Lodging House in Crum Hill provided a large rough table and stools downstairs while upstairs lodgers slept fully clothed on the floor. A 'washing line' was provided on which a garment could be put as a pillow. Street entertainers used it to appear poor, although they had good homes in other towns.

There is evidence of Terminating Building Societies, one sponsored by John Brunner. Money was invested by each member weekly. Land was purchased and houses started to be built. A lottery was drawn as each was completed to decide who it should be allocated to. When all the houses were built and paid for, the society wound-up or terminated.

An interesting community was Navigation Road, built for the Navigation workers. One block had the name Temperance Terrace picked out in blue bricks a yard high (it was obliterated by cladding in the 1970s). This illustrates the control of employers over workers outside working hours. Many Victorians believed that alcohol was the cause of poverty; the inscription proclaimed the houses were the benefit of sobriety, which was encouraged by the Trustees.

Pubs abounded in areas which were developed in a piecemeal fashion. Navigation Road and Winnington were 'dry' areas where pubs were prohibited. Much of Northwich, especially around Greenall's Road, was developed by the Greenall family of Warrington, brewers. As recently as 1976 every public house in the Urban District was owned by Greenall Whitley.

A significant housing development was the creation of a model factory community in Winnington from the 1880s. Brunner Mond needed to house their workers as the works were a distance from the town. It possesses little of the architectural grandness of Port Sunlight or Saltaire, but is nonetheless as significant a part of social history. The Company provided houses, schools, social club, library, a church but no pub.

Thomas Moreton, owner of Moss Farm, built Moreton and Appleton Streets and erected a building to be a pub between them. The company purchased it as a private house to prevent workers drinking. A bar in the Social Club was only achieved by challenging Brunner's convictions; as a member of a committee to reform pubs, arguing that he should trust his workers to do what he advocated.

The houses in Solvay Road and surrounding streets had reasonable rooms and a yard with a wash-house. They had outside 'earth closets' where a box above the seat was filled with ashes from the fire. A layer of ash was shaken from a box to cover the contents after use. Nightsoil men were employed to empty them during the night every week until mains sewers were provided in the 1950s. The two square openings, now bricked up, can be seen in the rear walls. The upper door was to load the ashes, the lower for the container to be emptied. The houses did not have bathrooms. Free shower and locker facilities were provided with drying rooms for clothes from 1901 but most preferred to use a tin bath on the hearth.

The houses in Dyar Terrace are said to be the first ever built from breeze blocks as an experiment, recycling furnace linings. Dyar, Hammond and Solvay were pioneers of the soda ash industry.

Brunner Mond's influence on housing extended beyond Winnington. Selected workers had favourable mortgages arranged through the Winnington Co-operative Society (founded in a Brunner Mond building in 1883), to build new houses at Hill Top Farm, Barnton. Many did not understand mortgages and it was rumoured that they were so much in debt that they could only afford 'jam butties' for Sunday dinner. Barnton is still called 'Jam Town'. During the 19th century the population of Northwich expanded beyond the old manors. The smoke, linked with the risk of fires, floods and subsidence made it desirable, for those who could afford it, to live out of town.

The move to Hartford started in the 18th century, with the Marshall family. The second Thomas purchased Greenbank Manor and his sons built Whitehall and Hartford Beach as country houses. Development along Chester Road was well established by the 1880s when the 'good houses' were commented on. They increased following the establishment of Brunner Mond. Managers had to live within ten minutes of their work-place in case of emergency. Middle-class houses for large families and servants to look after them were erected at Greenbank and Hartford. Their large gardens, tended by employed gardeners, provided food for the kitchen and pleasure grounds. The stations were convenient and it was down-wind of the factories.

Brunner Mond built many houses for its workers, and in 1983 almost 300 such dwellings were sold to tenants. Prefabricted four bedroomed bungalows — called 'Tin Town' — were built from 1907 by Brunner Mond as quick emergency workers' accommodation near The Avenue at Winnington. They had timber frames covered in corrugated iron and a central brick chimney-stack providing a fireplace in each of four rooms. They were occupied until the 1950s. The same year Brunner Mond petitioned the UDC to provide more houses as the works were expanding and needed to offer reasonable homes to attract skilled workers.

Significant housing estates at Rudheath and Owley Wood away from risk of subsidence were designed and built by the Rural District Council on Brunner Mond land. They were started in 1920. Acts introduced by Neville Chamberlain in 1923 and Lord Wheetley in 1924 allowed local authorities to borrow money to provide housing where there were shortages. The funding came partly from this source and the Rural Council, but also from Brunner Mond. They gave the largest sum given by any industrial concern to a local authority under the schemes. Most workers had bicycles and the estates were a short ride from the works and the development of the motor 'bus network made it easy to get to shops.

Built in Garden City style with gardens for vegetables, the estates at Rudheath, Owley Wood and 'The Golf Links' (Winnington) are important land-marks of housing development. They amply fulfilled the war-time promise of 'Homes fit for heroes'. They were among the largest developments in any rural parish; Weaverham and Barnton held records for the largest populated villages in England. By contrast Marbury had the smallest population in 1977; when it merged with Marston there were just 14 inhabitants, including two children.

After the Second World War Weaverham became an overspill town. Families left Liverpool with the promise of a house and a job at ICI. Leftwich Estate was built by the Urban District Council within the Rural District. The Urban boundary was extended to the by-pass to include them in 1955. Grass-verged roads and open spaces added to the attraction.

In 1951 the Gas Board congratulated the Northwich Rural District Council in local advertisements for 'leading the country in the number of post-war houses built'. The RDC housing stock that year was 3,193 houses and 350 'bungalows converted from military hutments'.

Recent housing development in Northwich was restricted to infilling smaller sites in the town centre as much land is unstable for building because of subsidence.

These developments and changes in industry influenced the nature of the population. Opportunities for casual work in salt works ended. The move from slum clearance during the inter-war years was headed by Canon Maitland Wood of Witton Church, an Urban District Councillor. He met with considerable hostility from those making money from renting sub-standard accommodation and those who had never known any other way of life. Others did not approve of subsidising houses from the rates. A float promoting the idea of slum clearance and ideal homes was even banned from appearing in the carnival.

Housing preference was given to people working with ICI, who had provided funding for the Council developments. By the middle of the 20th century much of the population around Northwich was directly or indirectly involved with ICI as it was almost a company town. Manual workers followed fathers and grandfathers to the 'Chimic', gaining council homes when they married. They had good company pensions when they retired.

Management also took a commitment to Brunner Mond for life; only after the advent of ICI did they start to move from town to town as they gained promotion. The population became stable, receiving good and regular wages with skilled workers living around the town and management to the west. Young and single people have been offered council houses in Winsford by Vale Royal Council since 1974, continuing this trend.

Today the Beehive pub is the only building residentially occupied in the old township of Northwich. The former Crown and Wateman's Arms (under new names) are the only occupied homes in the mediaeval area of Witton. They are the sole survivors of the dozens of pubs which once abounded in the town centre.

Only two miles away from the dirty slums of Northwich Rowland Egerton Warburton and his son Piers completely rebuilt the village of Great Budworth from the 1870s. They reused old materials, inspired by the Romantic Movement and the revival of English vernacular styles, as an attempt to capture a 'lost golden age' before industrialisation. Between the mock Tudor cottages (which use genuine old timbers) their architect, John Douglas, placed incredibly modern buildings for the time. Douglas owned Sandiway Manor and worked on the Duke of Westminster's villages besides many buildings in Sandiway and Whitegate. He was a pioneer of reviving traditional styles and adapting them to Victorian needs, as when he added tall chimneys copied from Tudor mansions to small cottages to allow for coal fires.

Great Budworth was a fore-runner of Tudor revivals and other rural housing schemes in the 1920s and '30s. Built for tenants on the Arley Estate it was neglected after the two sons were killed in World War I. In 1948 tenants were able to buy their cottages but from the 1970s the old families sold to wealthy newcomers and moved out. It forms the back-cloth to TV series like *Cluedo* and for adverts aimed at presenting a rose-coloured lens to old England.

ABOVE: There was better quality workers' housing in Timber Lane in 1892. (CL) BELOW: Working class dandies in white fustian trousers lounge about in Leicester Street, 1899. (CL)

ABOVE: Tin Town was built by Brunner Mond from 1907 as emergency workers' housing. (ICI) BELOW: 'Garden City' houses at Rudheath were built in pairs by the RDC from 1920. (NC)

LEFT: Dyar Terrace was built as separate villas for supervisors. (ICI) RIGHT: Victorian playground at Winnington's own school. (ICI) BELOW: Opening of Winnington's magnificent social club and cricket pavilion. (ICI)

133

LEFT: Sandiway's round tower was occupied as a Lodge to Vale Royal before the by-pass was built (MH) RIGHT: A complete contrast to Northwich: Arley Hall gardens by Piers Egerton Warburton. (AE)
BELOW: John Douglas and Rowland Egerton Warburton created this Victorian dream of old England at Great Budworth. (AE)

Bloodsports to Beatles

Up to the mid-19th century the Maypole was set up in the middle of the Bull Ring. After the dancing it was greased with lard and a leg of mutton was awarded to whoever could climb it. The town bonfire blazed in the Bull Ring.

Bulls were baited there, chained by the ring in their nose to an iron ring set in the middle of the road. It was difficult and painful to defend themselves against dogs who were set to 'try' them. Butchers with blocks waited and butchered them on the spot. The worrying quickened the blood-flow, making tender, redder meat. In 1758 James Bentley and Thomas Barlow, butchers, were fined 3s 4d for 'exposing the carcase of a bull for sale without first having baited him'. Bull-baiting moved to Lock Street, where one dog survived after being tossed over the River. An advert for 1820 records a bull baited at the Bowling Green, Leftwich. All dogs were to have a brass collar, the baiting lasted from 4 to 5 pm and the owner of the best dog received 'a good dinner and a quart of ale'. A 'capte' (blindfold?) goose was provided for a wild-goose-chase; the one who took its head kept its carcase. There was a scramble after a greased piglet; the one who caught it kept it to fatten for winter meat and bacon.

An unfaithful wife had to 'ride the stang', being paraded through the streets tied on a donkey. Drunks or petty thieves provided entertainment sitting in the stocks, pelted with spoiled food from the market. The 1832 Reform Bill ended this. Often a dancing bear or other performing animal was exhibited. Squire Lee Townshend of Wincham Hall kept bears for baiting and quarrelled with the local gentry. One Christmas he invited them to dinner as if in reconciliation, showing them to an empty room. When they were assembled he released the bears in the room, laughing at elegantly dresed people clambering through the windows.

The Cock Hotels at Northwich and Great Budworth recall cock-fighting and Cockpit Lane still exists at Sandiway. In the 19th century there were often fights on Sunday afternoons, when the representatives of two areas battled until one could not continue. Disagreements were settled with bare fist or clog fights, attracting large and rowdy crowds. Officials from Witton Chapel patrolled the streets to ensure that shops did not open, but a watch was kept, allowing all sorts of forbidden activities to happen on Sunday.

The Cheshire Hunt originated when Sir Peter Warburton of Arley moved his pack of hounds to Sandiway in 1798. The Hon John Smith Barry of Marbury Hall kept a pack at Ruloe. He was the first Master of Foxhounds in Cheshire and his portrait still presides over hunt meetings at the Swan in Tarporley. His hound Bluecap won a fortune in a speed trial at Newmarket in 1765 against a dog owned by the master of the Quorn Hunt. He was fitted with a lead collar to slow him down or he would leave the other hounds and outrun the fox. Catching foxes was not the main reason for hunting, but the riding of horses over an unknown course to follow one. The Cheshire countryside changed in the 18th century.

Strip fields were enclosed into hedged ones and new areas were cultivated. Fox hunting replaced hare coursing as it provided opportunities for horses to jump hedges, fences, ditches and brooks. Special woods called 'coverts' were planted for foxes to breed. Hartford Common was a well known racecourse until it was enclosed by the second Thomas Marshall.

Circuses often visited Northwich. In 1897 a trailer containing circus lions overturned on Winnington Hill causing consternation. Elderly people remember circus elephants bathing in the Dane.

Northwich had livestock fairs, attracting entertainers, from mediaeval times on 10 April, 2 August and on 6 December (St Nicholas' Day) Christmas poultry was sold to fatten at home. During the 19th century Northwich became closely associated with fairgrounds. During the winter showmen families from travelling fairs used a site called The Fairground near New Warrington Road. James Dean, a resident there, was the first secretary of the Showman's Guild from 1891-93 and was its president three times. He organised fellow showmen into a trade association to resist the activities of protection racketeers, thugs, confidence tricksters and other criminals following fairs. They made travelling fairs safe and respectable with the variety of rides we know today and ensured that reasonable winter sites were available for showmen. His monument is in Witton Churchyard with other graves of well-known showman families. In 1972 they moved to a new site to make way for a rear access road.

Northwich had a Wakes Week. Sports recorded for 18 September 1821 include rowing across the Weaver, a cart horse race from the Crown Hotel to the top of Castle Hill and back, clog races, a spinning match for women (using their own wheels) and a thick porridge-eating contest for children. The races stated at 8.00 in the morning and at 8.00 the following day open-air breakfast was served in Crown Street. This consisted of ale, bread and cheese, thick porridge and treacle, red herrings, onions and tobacco. Lostock School log for 1863 records children missing because of Lostock Wakes (31 Aug) and Budworth Wakes (16 Nov).

In 1859 a Town Hall was provided by Joseph Jackson in the classical style. It had a room 60 ft x 40 ft which could be hired for assemblies, balls, concerts, lectures etc. It became unsafe because of subsidence and for half of the 20th century Northwich had no adequate public hall. Victorian dances were sometimes held in salt mines. During the 2nd World War the swimming pool at the baths could be boarded over, forming a dance floor for servicemen stationed in the area to meet local girls.

Organised sports date from the latter part of the 19th century. Inter-town football matches could not take place until the railway allowed teams to travel easily. Northwich Victoria came into being in 1874 when Stedman College at Comberbach challenged a group of Northwich men to a game under Association rules. Men got together prior to that, playing rugby and 'soccer' between themselves. The two captains had learnt the rules at college. Sir John Deane's taught rugby from that period up to its conversion to a Sixth Form College despite requests repeated over many years from the Urban District Council. They argued that Northwich had two Association Clubs to recruit ex-pupils if only they knew how to play.

A division around Leicester Street separated Witton Albion and Vic's supporters, who met every year on Boxing Day and Easter Monday in matches attended by most of the town. There were many other local teams by the 1880s.

The original field called Stumpers was on the corner of Chesterway and London Road. The Pavilion Theatre, replaced by the Regal Cinema, was on part of it. The history of the Theatre in Northwich goes back at least until the 1820s when plays were performed in the Court House by the Town Bridge.

In 1874 Vics arranged to use the better facilities at the Drill Field. This was used by the Cheshire Rifle Volunteers for annual camps. Hundreds of men from all over Cheshire spent several days under canvas for training, including the use of heavy artillery pulled by horses. The land was given by Colonel Thomas Marshall, the last of the family involved with salt.

Conditions for football were far from ideal by today's standards. The 1875 OS Map has 'land liable to flood' printed on the field. A deep ditch was on two sides, so close to the touchline that corner kicks were taken from a plank across it. Goal posts were two poles like fishing rods with a piece of tape for the cross-bar. Games were often halted in bad weather for the referee to adjust the tape or posts after players crashed into them. The field was leased to circuses or agricultural shows which did not help to keep good turf.

After matches players walked to pubs to change and for refreshments. However, the Drill Field is recognised as the oldest field in the world on which Association Football has been continuously played.

In 1878, Victoria held a meeting at Hartford with representatives from Macclesfield, Crewe, Hartford and Wincham to form the Cheshire Association. In 1885, having won the Cheshire Cup for all of its six years they were allowed to keep it on display in the Museum room at the Library. On 9 February 1884 they were beaten in the quarter-final of the FA Cup by Blackburn Olympic. The Blackburn field was a quagmire and the ball was lost in liquid mud. There was no provision to cancel but protests forced the FA to change the rules.

Northwich Victoria played in the Second Division when it was formed in 1892. They abandoned this in 1894 as players could neither afford the fares nor the time for distance games. The fact that they were also the first League team to lose *all* their away matches influenced them to return to amateur status. They were founder-members of the Cheshire League in 1919 and the Northern Premier League in 1968.

Cricket locally seems to have started in villages where there was more open land, but no early records survive.

Swimming was provided at the Brine Baths in Verdin Park, where the concentration of brine made floating easy. From 1887. The Verdin Swimming Club was formed. They organised races in the Weaver for the 1897 Jubilee along with a water polo match. This culminated when two men, one in an evening suit, the other in a gown, dived fully clothed from the top of the Town Bridge. Technically this was illegal. Legislation ensuring free flow of traffic, never revoked, imposed a sentence of transportation on anyone swimming in the Weaver.

Whit Monday was the day for the Northwich Regatta, organised by the Rowing Club. For the 1897 Diamond Jubilee they organised a River Carnival of boats illuminated with more than 4,000 coloured glass jars, each containing a lighted candle. An illuminated steam barge, pulling a barge containing the Adelaide Band, headed the parade. Barges decorated with Japanese lanterns lined the river bank.

Cyclists' clubs existed in Northwich, Barton, Winnington and Lostock, and organised a parade of decorated cycles, ridden by people in fancy dress for the opening of the Technical Schools. Cycles were a fashion craze of the time and a cycle was a token of working class achievement before motor cars were common.

There were often garden parties in the grounds of country houses, usually to raise money for charity. A Fancy Fair in 1874 raised money towards building Hartford Church. Held in a field in front of the Manor, there were stalls selling items including products of Hartford's blacksmith or trinkets from Japan, plus sideshows and brass bands, with dancing until 9.00 pm. Special trains carried people from all local stations and Northwich shops closed for the afternoon as all customers were expected to be at the fair. Sometimes the reception rooms of Vale Royal, Bostock, Arley and Marbury Halls were opened to view the art collections for charity.

Indoor gymnastics were provided from 1897 with a gymnasium as part of the Verdin Technical Schools. This has a large stained glass window with representations of sports and a balcony from which spectators could watch.

Winnington Park Recreation club was founded in 1890 for workmen. A cricket ground was set out, surrounded by a track for running and cycle races, bowling greens, football and Rugby fields. A pavilion for changing and refreshments were added.

In 1896 the committee asked permission from the board of Brunner Mond to provide beer or stout but not spirits. They reported that many carried bottles to the club to drink after a game of bowls, while others preferred to pay to use the green in Verdin Park than go to near-by pubs. They wrote 'some of us, like the Bishop of Chester, think that they could manage a public house in such a way that it would not be a nuisance to the neighbourhood in which it stood'. This was a challenge to Brunner, who served on a committee chaired by the Bishop, aimed at reforming public houses. Brunner's views on temperance ensured that no public house was established in Winnington. The argument won the day and a small bar was provided. A new pavilion including stands and a bar was opened by Ludwig Mond in 1901.

Several pubs had crown bowling greens as did the Liberal (Gladstone) and Conservative Clubs. The former was built by the Library by public subscription, headed by Sir John Brunner. It contained several billiard tables on the first floor until destroyed by fire in suspicious circumstances during 1977. Billiard tables were included in all the Brunner Mond social clubs and Winnington Hall, in the Victoria (Masonic) Club and there were commercial billiard rooms in Church Road.

Northwich was the last town in Cheshire to keep an extra hour's drinking for market days. It lost Saturday after police objections in 1975 because young people from other pubs flocked to the market area, but retained Friday until afternoon closing ended.

After the donation of the Infirmary, the Working Men's Hospital Sunday was held in the Park from 1888 to raise funds. Most people worked on Saturday at that time. By the 1920s Saturday afternoons had been granted away from work and a less restrained entertainment could be provided. This developed into the Carnival parade on the first Saturday in July, with troupe dancing, a fair and the parade of visiting queens as we know it today. The first procession was held in 1927, with Marjorie Rayner as Queen. Northwich had such prestige among dance troupes that numbers were limited so they could all perform before nightfall.

In 1963 the Carnival Committee invited the Beatles, who had appeared on TV, to crown the Queen so as 'to attract youngsters'. Between the invitation and the Carnival they topped the charts. Black-haired Kathryn Millington was chosen and, true to a tradition that it rains if the Queen has black hair, it rained for three hours and the dance competition was abandoned. When the group appeared for the ceremony, crowds of teenage girls surged forwards to get closer to them and the crowning had to be abandoned. That evening the Memorial Hall was full to capacity to see them. Windows were opened so that hundreds outside could join in dancing in the rain. It was one of the first instances of what became known as 'Beatlemania'.

The Victory Memorial Hall was erected as the town's War Memorial after the 2nd World War. During that time morale had been kept high by dances, with many American servicemen from camps at Byley or Marbury attending. The Fairground site remained open throughout the War for servicemen and women. People agreed that once the war was over a good dance hall was a priority. The Memorial Hall opened on 1 June 1960. During the Swinging '60s chart-topping groups appeared there almost weekly. Special late 'buses took dancers to most Cheshire towns after the dances ended. It was built in sections on steel foundations, to withstand subsidence. A small gap near the emergency door opens over several years as the stage end sinks. After a time it is jacked up and the gap closes.

As people moved away from the town centre during the present century some traditions have been lost. A platform was erected in the Bull Ring, with choirs and the Salvation Army band, assembled to lead carol and other community singing, as Witton Church bells rang in the New Year. Walking Days from the Sunday Schools were also held.

The Barnton band is the only survivor of several brass and silver bands which once existed in and around Northwich and played at many functions. The traditional concerts and *Messiah* performed by the Festial Choir still attract large crowds.

Almost vanished from the local scene is the soulcaking tradition. Once this was performed in all local communities, now only surviving at Antrobus, but performed in various pubs around Budworth, building up to All Souls Day on 2 November. It links to the Celtic worship of the horse goddess Epona, and the performers represent the souls of the local dead. The idea of providing food for them goes back to ancient times. It starts with a battle when King (originally Saint) George killed the Black (faced) Prince. After this a man dressed as a woman would appear as the Prince's mother. She was derived form bisexual Celtic divinities and asked a doctor — originally a druid — to restore the prince to life. This was followed by a mock auction of a horse, which was a painted horse's skull supported on a single 'leg' and wired so the jaw snapped. The battle, shedding of blood and restoration of life is derived from pagan ideas of seasonal sacrifice, death and restoration of life in nature. The Moulton Crow Dance has similar origins in fertility rites. In such traditions, which were never written down, but passed verbally down the generations, we find the origins of British theatre.

Since 1976, the development of the arts in Northwich, better known as DAN, has promoted a wide variety of events around the town, many sponsored by Arts Council grants and the Town Council. This has included classic theatre, music, and events which explore avant-garde art forms.

The first season ticket of Northwich Vics, 1884. (ICI)

To be non-partisan, here are ABOVE: Northwich Victoria and BELOW: Witton Albion before World War I. (MB)

ABOVE: Shin pads were a new invention when Cheshire Lad's team wore one each. (MB) BELOW: This team of women munition workers (1914-18) wears Albion shirts. (NC)

LEFT: The infamous goals on the Drill Field. RIGHT: The Pavilion Theatre was built on the 'Stumpers' ground and replaced by the Regal Cinema. (NC) BELOW: The State Theatre was unfinished when World War II broke out and remained so for half a century. (NC)

ABOVE: The Beatles were asked to leave the stage at the Carnival in 1963. (NC) BELOW: Besses O'Th'Barnton Band in 1900. (NC)

ABOVE: Barnton Band, here in 1908, was one of several workers' brass bands. (NC) BELOW: Barnton Cycling Club, 1881. (NC)

ABOVE: Northwich Swimming Club, 1918. (NC) BELOW: Scenic Dragons from Collins Fair, which wintered in Northwich, at the Winington Works Jubilee. (ICI)

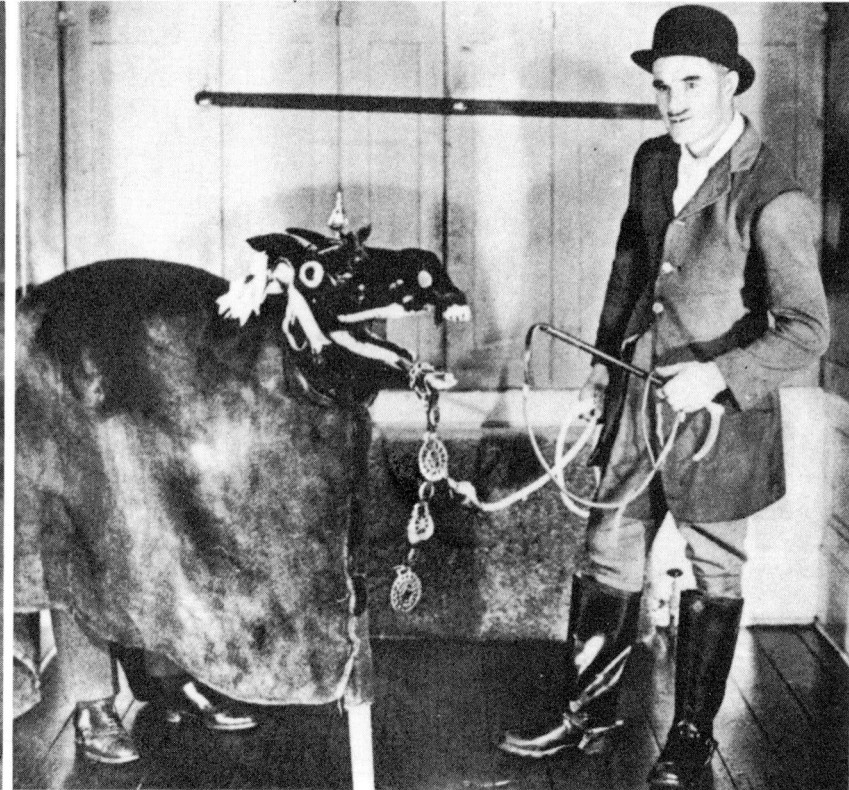

ABOVE: Golden Jubilee of Winnington Works; six tents served everyone with tea together. (ICI) LEFT: Memorial to James Dean, founder of the Showman's Guild, in Witton Churchyard. (SP) RIGHT: The wild horse and driver of the Antrobus Soulcakers, 1946.

ABOVE: Edward Evans the Ostler at Roberts' Bakery in 1920. (RB)
RIGHT: Roberts' first motor-van in 1929. (RB) BELOW: Roberts' delivery vans in 1959. (RB)

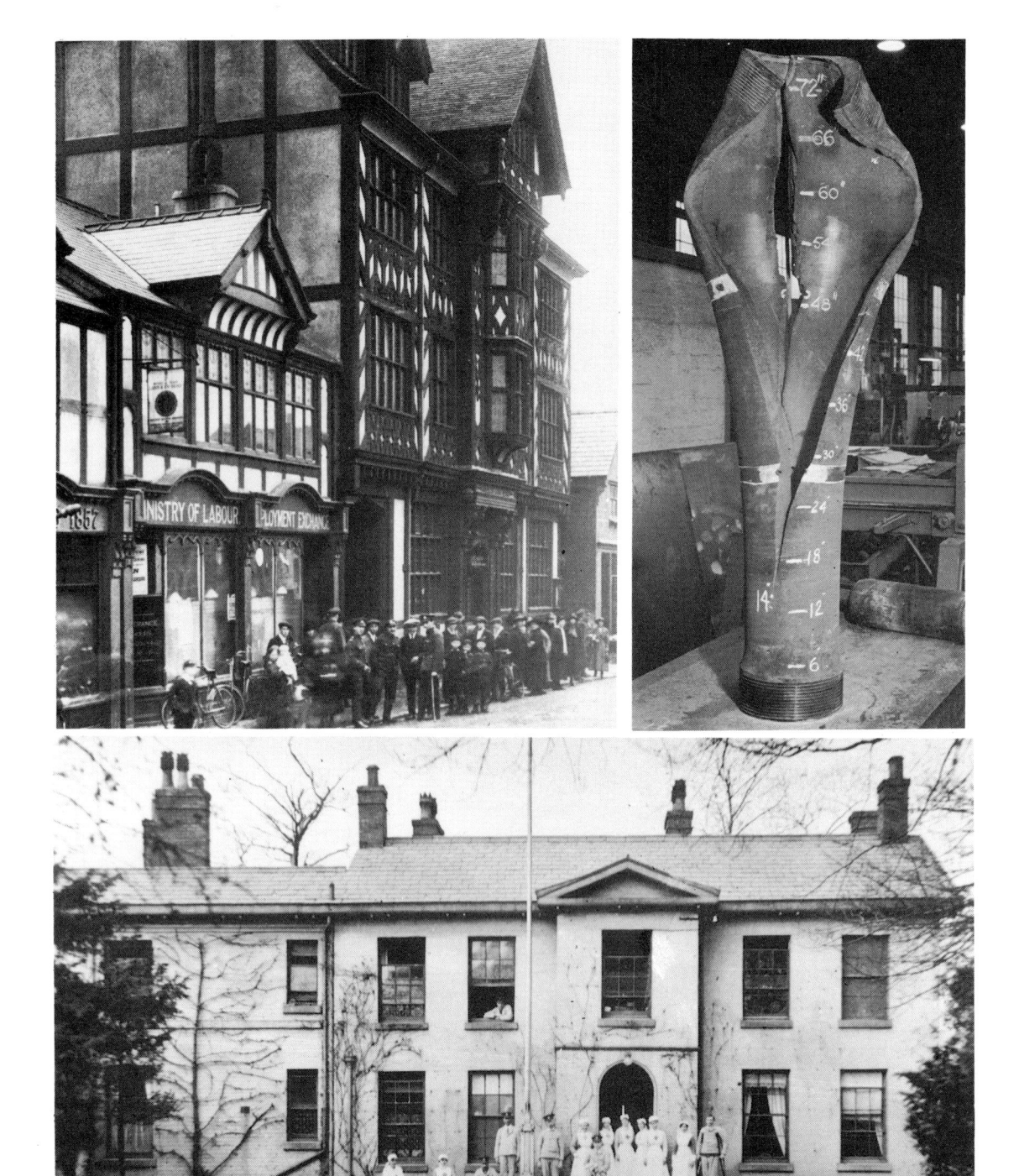

LEFT: After World War I, soldiers with walking sticks joined others in the dole queue. (NC) BELOW: The Lee Red Cross Hospital, Winnington provided care for wounded World War I soldiers (NC) RIGHT: Heating ethylene under high pressure to make polythene often caused equipment to explode. (ICI)

They Changed Our Lives

The year of the General Strike, 1926, is better remembered locally for the formation of ICI (Imperial Chemical Industries Limtied) which started to trade on 1 January 1927. This came about because of competition from large American and German concerns posing a threat to British trade. Problems of chemical production experienced in the 1914-18 War highlighted this. One mighty concern resulted as Brunner Mond merged with Nobel Industries, British Dyestuffs Corporation and United Alkali Company.

The merger was tainted with tragedy. Sir John Brunner's son, Roscoe, was expected to take a leading role in the new Company. The story of his suicide is linked to the supply of soda to soap companies. Lever's of Port Sunlight were Brunner Mond's biggest customer.

Problems started in 1911 when Levers purchased land on salt beds at Lymm to produce their own soda. Brunner Mond retaliated, buying Levers' leading competitors, Crossfield and Gossages. William Lever, who loved law-suits, took them to litigation, forcing them to sell these soap-making interests to him for £4 million.

After the 1914-18 War Lever's agreed a price-increase, on condition that the Co-operative Wholesale Society paid a higher price. They refused. Confusion followed as J. C. Nicholson left the country after telling Company Secretary, J. H. Gold, that he had reached an agreement with Lever. For four years the two contracts ran side by side, with Lever ever-more suspicious about CWS prices. Roscoe Brunner's nerve broke and on 31 March 1924 he revealed the situation in a letter to Lever, who prepared to sue. Alfred Mond was advised that Brunner Mond had no case and to settle out of court for damages of one million pounds.

Brunner was hurt and depressed and his was not one of the names Brunner Mond nominated for places on the Board of ICI. He resigned on grounds of ill-health, refusing to comment and retreating to his London home. His wife, Ethel, tried to put her husband's point of view to the press. She was furious as the whole blame seemed to be put on him.

The day her comments appeared (3 November 1926) he shot her. She was found by the door in outdoor clothes. A car was waiting for them outside. He put his arm around her body and, sitting in a loving embrace, shot himself.

The story of the agreement forming ICI is like an episode from a thriller. The chief British players were Sir Alfred Mond and Sir Harry McGowan of Nobel Industries. Both went to New York to negotiate independently with Orlando F. Weber, head of the American Allied Chemical and Dye Company or Dr Carl Bosch, the head of the German IG Teerfabriken. Negotiations were conducted behind locked doors. Both British firms wanted an alliance with either of the foreign companies but negotiations were difficult.

Disillusioned, McGowan approached Mond with a proposal to merge their enterprises with the two other British companies. The proposal was agreed by Brunner Mond's negotiators next day. The settlement with Lever's left Brunner Mond short of money to invest in developing the nitrate fertilizer industry, the result of work on explosives at Lostock in the war. Nobel's provided the ready money and knowledge of explosives that was needed. Much of Brunner Mond's capital had been used to build Wallerscote Works, which started production on Christmas Day, 1926.

The two parties returned to Britain on the *Aquitania* on 6 October, agreeing details of the merger on the way. Typed on four sheets of the ship's headed notepaper it is known as 'The Aquitania Agreement'. McGowan suggested that the new company should be called Brunner's but Imperial Chemical Industries was agreed as they expected to trade within the British Empire, the largest trading network then known.

ICI started business on 1 January 1927. Sir Alfred Mond was the first Company Chairman, with McGowan as Deputy and President of the Board. Alfred was the second son of Ludwig Mond and studied law at Cambridge; he copied Brunner's business methods. Like him he had served as an MP and was Minister of Health in 1921-2. He was involved at Government level in the creation of the state of Israel. He returned to the board of the Company after the fall of the Coalition Government, just in time to take over from Roscoe Brunner. Elevated to the House of Lords he used the title Lord Melchett. The local works became a division of ICI under the title Alkali Division, later the Mond Division in his honour.

One of the most significant events after the merger was the discovery of polythene in the Winnington Research Laboratores. Reginald O. Gibson was researching the effects of high pressures using ethylene. He recorded in his note book 'waxy solid found in reaction tube' on 27 March 1933. Commercial production began, significantly, the day Hitler invaded Poland, 1 September 1939.

The Fuehrer attributed British superiority in the Battle of the Atlantic and other victories to polythene. Used an an anti-static insulator for radar it enabled the British to out-manoueuvre the Germans.

There was another link with wartime radar. Just before he died, Lawrence of Arabia (Col T. E. Lawrence) worked in Northwich on a small radio-controlled spy vessel, built in top-secret at Yarwoods' boatyard. It was successfully used in the Second World War and as a prototype for others. He stayed at the Crown and Anchor under his false name, Shaw.

In 1939 the total production of polythene was 10 tons. In 1944 1,400 tons was produced, mostly for military use. After the war people became used to things, from buckets to raincoats, marketed under the brand name *Alkathene* by the Alkali Division. Polythene (polymerised ethylene) is made by heating ethylene under great pressure, which often caused explosions heard all over the district.

One research project had profound effects on the post-war era. The Research Laboratories conducted work on uranium and nuclear fission as part of a coordinated wartime effort with universities, leading to the British nuclear bomb. ICI was invited to join the project as there would be need for production on an industrial scale. The research was undertaken with belief in the peaceful use of nuclear energy as a fuel after the war. Working under top-secret conditions they avoided suspicion, using the name 'Directorate of Tube Alloys', on the principle that everything scientific uses tubes. It sounded important enough not to create undue curiosity about scientists working in what was called the High Pressure Lab.

At one stage the British project was ahead of the Americans. After the war ICI employee Michael Perrin emulated Freath's expedition to Germany, recruiting ten leading scientists, who worked on nuclear fission under Hitler, to join the British team. Churchill believed the balance of post-war power would rest with holders of nuclear weapons and without it Britain would become a second-class state.

After the Second World War ICI found employment for numerous Polish refugees who had settled in camps at Marbury and Delamere. Some with high academic qualifications accepted labouring posts as poor English made communication difficult, but achieved responsible positions as their English improved. Their children were recruited into all levels within the company, many as graduates.

It is appropriate, having considered artificial fertilizers, polythene and nuclear fission, to record a fourth great wartime development. The jet engine was perfected at Wincham, though not by ICI.

Frank Whittle hit upon the idea as a 22-year-old cadet. His superiors ridiculed it because of his youth. Senior aircraft production officials had shares in factories producing piston engines. The Government refused to take out a patent. When war broke out, Germany produced jet engines and had aircraft flying before Britain did.

Work started just after the outbreak of war to produce a British engine at the Metropolitan-Vickers factory in Trafford Park, which was soon hit by a bomb. The General Manager of the works was Albert Stubbs, Chairman of the New Cheshire Salt Works at Wincham.

He offered use of land there away from likely bombing, where work could continue. The Ministry of Aircraft Production set up a factory where the engines could be built. It has a plaque to record that engines for the world's first jet-propelled sea-plane and gas turbine-driven boat were tested there between 1940 and 1949. Testing took place in secret but the noise was heard at great distance, giving rise to many rumours. The engine was perfected under the direction of Dr David Smith and was an improvement on Whittle's idea, which worked on a centrifugal principle, expelling air from the engine sides. The improved engine pushed air and ignited fuel down a narrowing tube. The Government gave all specifications and retail rights to America, as a bribe to encourage them to join the war, so that the inventor and perfectors did not receive a penny royalties.

Half a century later jet planes fly above Northwich every few minutes on the flight path to Manchester International Airport.

Marbury Hall, copy of Fontainebleu by Salvin, housed Dunkirk survivors, then PoWs and Polish refugee workers for ICI. (NC)

152

Postscript

On 1 April 1974 Local Government Reorganisation saw the creation of Vale Royal Borough Council. Its boundaries were drawn for political purposes, linking Northwich and Winsford with Frodsham and Tarporley, with which there were no traditional links. Middlewich, with which there had always beenk links, was given to Congleton and Plumley, the source of ICI's brine, was given to Macclesfield. The Urban District Council became the Town Council, with limited responsiblity, but was allowed to have a Mayor for the first time, with Cllr Barry Rose as the first to hold that office.

Northwich is situated near the centre of the new County of Cheshire. Green Hill at Whitley between Northwich and Warrington was chosen by the Ordnance Survey as the point nearest to the centre of mainland Britain, from which all maps spread outward and it is conveniently situated for the cities of Manchester, Liverpool and Stoke.

In 1991 policy within ICI had changed and the Company felt the need for increasing specialisation. The salt and soda ash concerns were sold. The old names of Brunner Mond and the Salt Union were revived, heralding the start of a new era in Northwich history.

Only a few miles away near Pickmere one of the satellite telescopes of Jodrell Bank now traces events in space which occurred before the salt beds were laid down.

OPPOSITE: Metropolitan Vickers engine, type F/24, on test at Wincham in January, 1945. (NCSW) BELOW: The 'High Pressure Labs' at Winnington, where research into nuclear weapons was conducted. (ICI) ABOVE: Model of the Town Centre Development, 1962.

Bibliography

Axon, W. E. A. *Cheshire Gleanings,* Axon, 1884.
Beamont, William, (translator), *Domesday Book for Lancashire and Cheshire,* Minshull & Hughes, 1893.
Barker, T. C. *Lancashire Coal and Cheshire Salt and the Rise of Liverpool,* Lancs & Ches Historic Soc 1951
Bagley, J. J. *A History of Lancashire,* Philimore, 1976.
Bagshaw, S. *Directory and Gazeteer of Cheshire,* 1850.
Binney, W. H. *Parish Church (Northwich), Witton Church.*
Brunner, John T. and Ellis T. E. *Public Education in Cheshire,* 1890.
Bolger, Paul *The Cheshire Lines Committee,* Heyday, 1984.
Buchan, G. H. Barnton, *A Portrait of Times Past,* 1988.
Burd, Van Atkin *The Winnington Letters of John Ruskin,* George Allen & Unwin, 1969.
Calvert, A. G. *Salt in Cheshire,* 1915.
Chaloner, W. H. *Salt in Cheshire 1600-1870,* Lancs and Chesh Historic Soc, 1961.
  The Cheshire Activities of Matthew Boulton and James Watt, Lancs and Cheshire Antiquarian Soc, 1949.
Cheshire Women's Institutes, *Cheshire Village Memories,* 1952.
Collins, Jill & Penny, Stephen, *Anderton Basin,* Cheshire County Council, 1989.
Cooke John H. *Bibliotheca Cestrensis,* Mackie, 1904.
  The Queen's Diamond Jubilee in Cheshire, Mackie, 1899.
Cox, Marjorie, *A History of Sir John Deane's Grammar School,* Manchester University Press, 1975.
Crump, W. B. *Saltways from the Cheshire Wiches,* Lancs & Chesh Antiquarian Society, 1939.
Davies, J. W. Methodism in Hartford, Hartford Methodist Church, 1983.
Dick, W. L. F. *A Hundred Years of Alkali in Cheshire,* ICI, 1972.
Dickinson, Joseph, *The Landslips in the Salt Districts of Cheshire,* HM Inspectorate of Mines, 1872.
Dodgson, J. McNeil, *Place Names of Cheshire,* Cambridge University Press, 1970.
Eddison, Mike, *A Little Gem,* Cheshire County Libraries, 1985.
Edwards, R. K. *A Team For All Seasons,* (Northwich Victoria), Cheshire Country Publishing, 1992.
Foster, Charles, Arley Hall, 1982.
Hodson, J. H. *Cheshire 1660-1780,* Cheshire Community Council, 1978.
Hoole, Christina, *Traditions and Customs of Cheshire,* Williams & Norgate, 1937.
Hughes, G.A. *The Early Days of the Vics,* Northwich Victoria, 1931.
Harries, Michael & Lynch, Colin J. *An Illustrated History of Northwich Parish and Church,* Heritage Committee, 1981.
Head, Sir George *A Tour through the Manufacturing Districts of England,* 1835.
Hewitt, H. J. *The Buildings of the Railways of Cheshire,* Moreton, 1972.
Hughes, Herbert *Cheshire and its Welsh Border,* Dobson, 1966.
Goodman, Jean *The Mond Legacy,* Weidenfield & Nicholson, 1982.
Iredale, D. A. *The Rise and Fall of the Marshalls of Northwich.* Historic Society of Lancashire and Cheshire, 1965.
Irvine, A. S. *Winnington Hall,* ICI, 1951.
  The Story of Salt, ICI, 1962.
  Winnington Works At Home, ICI, 1965.

Jones, G. D. B. *Condate, Roman Northwich*, Archaeological Journal, 1972.
  Roman Manchester, Sherratt, 1974.
Kelly, *Directory of Cheshire*, 1906.
Koss, Stephen E. *Sir John Brunner, Radical Plutocrat*, Cambridge University Press, 1970.
Lavell, Paul *A Hundred Years of Recreation*, Winnington Park Recreation Club, 1990.
Lightfoot, T. S. *The Weaver Watermen*, Cheshire Libraries.
Lynch, Colin J. *Northwich in Times Past*, Countryside Publications, 1979.
  Northwich of Yesteryear, Cheshire County Publishing, 1986.
  Old Northwich, Cheshire Country Publishing, 1990.
  Various typescript and manuscript essays in the Northwich Library.
Newell, C. E. *The Brine Pumping* (Compensation for Subsidence Bill), 1891.
Nulty, Geoffrey *Guardian Country*, Cheshire County Newspapers, 1978.
Mattingly, H. (Translator), *Tacitus on Britain and Germany*, Penguin, 1948.
Mitford, Nancy *The Ladies of Alderley*, Chapman & Hall, 1938.
Morris, Christopher (Ed), *The Journeys of Celia Fiennes*, Cresset, 1946.
Murell, A. M. *John Henry Cooke*, Nichols & Co., 1963.
Northwich Chronicle, files of past editions.
Northwich Guardian, particularly information in 'The Market Place' column.
Northwich RDC *Tenant's Handbook*, 1952.
Northwich UDC, *Town Redevelopment Brochure*, 1962.
Northwich Heritage Society *I Remember*, 1993.
Paget Tomlinson, Edward *Mersey and Weaver Flats*, Wilson.
Penant, E. H. Douglas (& others) *Penrhyn Castle*, National Trust, 1991.
Piggot, J. *Directory of Cheshire*, 1828.
Reader, W. J. *Imperial Chemical Industries, Vol 1*, 1970.
  Imperial Chemical Industries, Vol 2, 1975.
Richards, Raymond *Old Cheshire Churches*, Moreton, 1947.
Rochester, Mary *Salt In Cheshire*, (three teachers' packs) Cheshire County Council.
Rochester, Mary and others, Brochures on *History of Salt*, Cheshire County Libraries and Museums.
  NSPCC Mid-Cheshire Branch Centenary History, 1968.
Frank Roberts & Sons *Centenary Brochure*, 1987.
Samuel, Raphel (Ed) *Miner Quarrymen and Saltworkers*, Routledge, Keegan & Paul, 1977.
Slater, George *Chronicle of Lives and Religion in Cheshire*, Crombie, 1891.
Smith, William & Webb W. *The Vale Royal of England*, Daniel King, 1656.
Sylvester, Dorothy & Nulty, Geoffrey *The Historical Atlas of Cheshire*, Cheshire Community Council, 1958.
Thompson, Hugh *Roman Cheshire*, Cheshire Community Council, 1964.
Ward, Thomas, Pamphlets on Salt, Guardian Office, 1874-84.
Walton, H. *Saint Luke's Church, Winnington*, 1959.
Ward, Thomas *Salt; an address at the opening of the Salt Museum*, Guardian Office, 1885.
Watts, John I. *The first Fifty years of Brunner Mond*, Brunner Mond, 1923.
Weaverham Local History Society *Old Weaverham*, Cheshire County Publishing.
Whitworth, Rev Clifford *Congragational Church, Northwich*, 1958.
White, Francis *Directory and History of Cheshire*, 1860.
Wiliams, Daniel *Illustrated Account of Northwich Congregational Church*, 1908.
Willan, T. S. *The River Weaver in the 18th Century*, Cheetham Society, 1951.
Winsford Local History Society *The River Weaver*, 1973.
Yarwood, Derek *Outrages Fatal and Otherwise*, Didsbury Press, 1991.

Index

All figures in *italics* refer to illustrations

Acton Bridge 39,55
Acts of Parliament
   Anderton Lift 57
   Brine Compensation ... 103
   Cheshire Salt Districts
      Compensation 114
   Combinations 80
   Conventicle 51
   Education 42
   Factory 93
   Housing 129
   Libraries & Museums . 102, 115
   Reform Bill 1832 ... 42,135
   Riot 101
   Sale of Northwich 38
   Swing Bridges 57
   Toleration 51
   Uniformity 31,51
   Watermen's Churches ... 53
   Weaver Navigation .. 17,36
Adelaide Band 137
   Mine 91,114
adult education 74
African salt trade 37
Agricola 17,19
Alderley 38
Alkoke, Richard . 24,43,52,53
Allostock 51
All Souls Day 139
American Allied Chemical & Dye Co 149
Anderton . 36,37,56,57,85,89
   Lift 72
Antelope 81
Antoninus Pius 18
Antrobus 139,*146*
Aquitania Agreement 150
Arkwright, Sir Richard . 35,37
Arley 28,55,130,135,137
   Hall *29*
Arts & Crafts
      Movement 1115,139
Ashton's Flashes 114
Ass-ociation cartoon *40*
Aston, Nicholas 31
   Sir Thomas 31
Atlantic, Battle of 150
Athelbrae *63*
Baptists 53
Barlow, Thomas 135
Barnton 61,76,91,129,137
   Band 139,*144*
   Town Brook 56
Barker, Daniel 51
Barnes, Isaac 52
Barons Croft 36,37
   Quay 37,43,52,53
   mine 80
Barrow family 36
BASF plant, Oppau 91
Bates 43,81
bear baiting 135
Beatles 138,*143*
Beeston 127
Belgium 89
Bell, Miss Margaret 75
bell pits 80,113
Bentley, James 135
   Dr William 31,*33*
Bernard, Sir Thomas 127

Big Freeze 58,65
Billinge Green *116*
Birkenhead, Sir John 33
biscuit-making 97
Bishop Jayne, of Chester . 76
Blackburn Olympic 137
blackleg labour 81
Black Greyhound 55
bleach packers 96,97
Bluecap 135
Blue Ribbon Army 53
boatbuilding *64*
Boer War 103
Booth, Sir George 32,*34*
Bosch, Carl 149
Bostock, A.W. 115
   Hall 37,137
Bosworth, Battle of 135
Bourne, Hugh 53
bowling green 135
Bowman Thompson &
   Co 90
Bracegirdle, Rev John . 73,77
Brat House 74
Brereton, Sir William .. 31,*34*
Bridge House 115,*123*
Bridgewater, Duke of .. 35,56
Brigantia 17
Brindley, James 37
Brine Baths 107,108,137
   formation 13,113
Brineseheath Brow 36
Britannia 23
British Association 80,103
   Dyestuffs Corpn 149
Broadhurst's Bakeries 91, 95,98,99
Brockhurst 103,*109*
Broome, Ralph 33
Broken Cross 18,37,56
Brook, Lady 95
Bronze Age 14
Brownshood, John 73
Bruen, John 73,74
Brunner, Ethel 149
   Jane 90
   (Sir) John T. ... 88,89 *et seq*, 95,101,102,*104*,114, *126,128*,138
   Library *109*
   Mond .... 44,53,58,*88*, 89 *et seq*,94,95,101,128, 130,*132*,138,149,150,153
   Roscoe 149,150
   Salome 90
   Sheilagh 91
Budworth 139
Bunsen, Prof 89
bull baiting 135
Bull Ring 52,105,115,*121*, 135,139
'bus services 67
Byley 138
Buxton 58,89,114
cake production 98
Calvin 51
canal *112*
Cape Farm 51
Cartimandua 17

carnival 105,138
Castle 14,17,18,23,24,36, 51,127
Catherine the Great 37
chambers *120,121*
Chancery 74
Cheshire Association 137
   Cup 137
   Hounds 103
   Hunt 135
   Lines Railway 12,58,59
      shunters 66
   Rifle Volunteers 136
Chester 18,55
   Bishop of 81,138
   Earls of 23,24
Chesters 18
child labour 44,93
chimic 130
chip shop *47*
cholera 41
Cholmondeley, Thomas .. 28, 32
churches, chapels etc
   Barnton 53
   Bourne Chapel 54
   Catholic 58
   Congregational 51
      Winnington 50
   Crown Street Chapel ... 51, 52,53
   Free 53
   Hartford 54,94,137
   Holmes Chapel 25,28
   Holy Trinity 53
   Leftwich *54*
   London Road 54
   Lostock Gralam 53
   St Paul's 53
   Tabernacle 53
   Tin Missions 53
   United Free 54
      Methodist 74
   Watermen's 50
   Witton 22,29,31,32,33, 51,127,130,135,136,139
Churchill 150
Civil War 31,32,51
Clarke, Edwin 57
Clive, Robert of India 74
Clowes, James 53
Coates, Mary 75
cockfighting 135
Cole, Lord 103
Conservative Club ... 102,138
   offices 101
Cooke, George Hatt 91
   J.H. 42
Coombe's Stores *45*
Coronation Day 51
Co-operative Wholesale
   Soc 149
Council House 76
courts 42
Crawford, James 53
Crawley, J. 115
Crimean War cannon *107*
Cromwell, Oliver 31,32
Crossfield, Sir Joseph .. 90,94

Crum Hill 27,126,128
Cut, the 27,52
cycling clubs 138,*145*
Cynosure 81
Dale, Moses 52
dairy industry 44
Dane Bridge *70*,89,115
   warehouse *45*,56
   River ... *12*,14,17,25,28,29, 36,37,56,79,114,136
Danish settlers 23
Darby, Abraham 36
Dark Ages 23
Davenham 53
Davey Faraday Research
   Labs 102
Dean, James 135,*145*
   Dr James 103
Deane, Sir John 27,73,76
   Lawrence 73
Defoe, Daniel 35
Delamere, (Lord)...90,103,150
Derby, Earl of 28,32,38
Devil's Kitchen 91
Dissenters 51,53
Dissolution 24
Disraeli 89
Domesday *21*,24
Done, John 25
Donkey Field 44
Douglas, John 53,130
Drakelow 25,37
Drill Hall 101
   Field 44,75,136,137
Dunnett, Mary 54
Dunkirk 113
Dutton 44
Earle, Peter 31
Eaton, Dr 74
Eddisbury Hundred 24
Edward I *108*
   VII 103,105,*108*
   Confessor, the 24
   Prince 23,27
Egerton Warburton,
   R. & P. 130
Elam's clock *47*
Ellis, Thomas Edward...76,101
elections *100*,104
Ellerton, K. 115
Enniskillen, Earl of .. 103,*108*
Ethelflaeda 23
Evans, Edward *147*
Factory Village 92
fairs 136,*145*
Fairground, the 136
Falk, Herman 80,93
Farm of the Good
   Shepherd 53
Fiennes, Celia 35
flat boats *85*
Flatmen's Assoc 80
floods 115,*118,124,125*
football 136,137
France-Hayhurst, Canon .. 41
Freath, Dr Francis 91
freebooters 38
furnaces 18
Fury's Mine 114
Fury Pond 114
Ford's Model Lodging
   House 128
foundries 43
Fusser, John le 25

General Strike 149
Gadbrook 52,91
Garden Bakeries 95
  City 129,*132*
Gas Board 129
Gibson, Reginald O. 150
Gibsons 43
Gladstone 101
  Club 102,*109*
Gorst family 43
Gold, J.H. 149
golf links 129
Grand Junction Railway ... 57
Gray, Michael 93
Great Budworth *14*,23,24,
  28,51,73,130
  Marston Mine 80,87
Greenhall family 128
  Rev Richard 53
  Whitley 128
Greenbank .. 37,42,45,90,129
  Manor 129
Grosvenor, Lord Henry . 102
  Museum 19
Guildhalls 95
Hadrian, Emperor 18
Halath Ddu, Halath Wen 23
Hallé, Sir Charles 75
Hand, Thomas 74
Happy Valley (Kenya) 103
Harbury Hall 39
Harden, Judge 42
Hardie, Keir 95
Harris's depôt 67
Harisson, Thomas 29
Hartford 28,32,36,37,42,
  45,51,53,57,90,127,129,
  137
  Bridge(s) *71*
  Common 136
  Grange 103
  Hall 91
  Station 19,55,89,103
Hayhurst Bridge 43,57
Hefferston Grange 37
Heidelberg 89
helmet 16
Helsby Hill 55
Heywood family 38,42
Higgins, Edward 55
High Sheriff 81,102
highwaymen 55
Hilltop Farm 129
Hitler 150
Holland, Henry 44
Holcrofts 28
Hole Hall 28
Holford Brine Field 90
  Hall 26,28
  Moss 51
Hornby, Pat 42
horsed traffic 46
  omnibus 59
Hospital Sunday 138
hotel, inns etc
  Beehive 130
  Bull's Head 48,55
  coaching inn 46
  Cock 48,135
  Crown 47,116,130,136,
    150
    Hotel 42,55,115
    Crown & Anchor 55,150
    Freemason's Arms 18

George & Dragon 53
Greyhound, Lostock 59
Leicester Arms 116
Lion & Railway Hotel ... 42
Nancollis Temperance
  Hotel 42
New Inn 116
Penryn Arms *49*
Queen's Head 74,76
Red Lion 51
Roebuck 116
Stanley Arms, Anderton..57
Saracen's Head, Chester..74
Swan 135
Talbot 77
Waterman's Arms .. *49*,130
Wheatsheaf *121*
White Lion 115
Witch & Devil 116
Hunter, Thomas 24
Hunts Lock 42,*61*
Hutchinson, John, & Co .. 89
Ice Age 13
ICI apprentices 78
  barges *62*
  Ltd 58,81,130,149,150,
    152,*153*
  steamer *63*
Industrial Revolution . 35,36,
  37
Infirmary 138
Irish workers 41
Ironbridge Museum 43
Jackson, Joseph 136
jacking points 115,*117*
Jam Town 129
James I 28,29
jet engine 151
Jodrell Bank 153
Jones, Thomas 74
Jubilees 41,101,102,138,
  145
Kaye, Thomas 74
Kent, Duke of 91
Kinderton 23,28,38
King, Daniel 28
Knutsford 23,56
Lagos salt 80
Lambert, General 32
Lamprey Brook 17
Latham Hall 27
Lawrence, T.E.
  (of Arabia) 150
lead ore 18
Le Blanc process 89
Le Cross 24,28
Leach End 27
  Eye 27
Leadbetter, Eliza 48
leadblockers 28
Leader-Williams, Edward....57
Lee family 28
Leftwich 27,28,41,42,44,
  52,53,*123*,129
  Hall 26
Leicester of Tabley 38,43
Lever Company 149
  William 149
Ley, Rev John 31
Liberal Club 138
Libraries 102,103,*106*,*110*,
  137,138
Lion Salt Works ... 81,85,103,
  114

Litchenstein, Prince
  Ferdinand de 91
Littlers Mine *40*
  Yard 43
Liverpool 41,45,81,89,94,
  103
  University 90,101
Livesay, James 31
Local Board 42,76,102
lock-up 42
Lodporne Stone 27
London 51,55
  Dockers' Strike 95
  North Western Railway....58
Lostock 51,53,55,90,91,95,
  124,127,137,149
  Hall *30*
Lothian, Major 31
Lowe, Romper 38
Lupus, Hugh 24
Macclesfield 137
Magic Methodists 54
Mainwaring(s) 95
Manchester 38,52,80
  Airport 151
  Ship Canal 57
Mann, Tom 95
manorial court 27
Marbury 35,*112*,116,129,
  138,150
  Hall 39,135,137,*151*
Margaret, Princess 91
markets 24,25,42
Market Hall 110
Marshall, Thomas I...36,74,75
  II 36,37,56,129,136
  Col Thomas H. 94,136
  Salt Works 56
Marrow, Col John 32
Marston 56,80,114,129
  Moor, Battle of 32
Martindale, Rev Adam . 23,31
Mary, Lady 28
McArdle, John 42
McGowan, Sir Harry..149,150
maypole 135
Melchett, Lord 150
Memorial Hall 37
Mercurius Aulicus 33
Mersey 81
Metcalf's Mine 52,56
Methodism 51,52,53
Metropolitan-Vickers 151
Middlewich .. 18,31,41,57,58,
  101,102
Milky Lime Dept 95
Milner, Edward 89
Millington, Kathryn 138
Ministry of Aircraft
  Production 151
Mitford, Nancy 38
Mond, Sir Alfred 149,150
  Frida 90,93
  Ludwig ...... 76,88,89 *et seq*,
    95,138,150
Monel 81
Moores, John 38
Moreton, Thomas 128
Mort, John 38
Moss Farm 128
Moulton Crow Dance 139
  Lord 91
Mow Cop 53
  Museum 137

Nantwich 29
  Gallery 102
narrow boats *64*,*65*
Neolithic 14
New Cheshire Saltworks .. 81
Newhall, William 25
Neuman's Flashes 80,114
Nicholas, Grand Duke 80
Nicholson, J.C. 149
Nickson, Thomas 33
Nigeria 80,81
Nixon, Robert 115
Nobel Industries 149
Norman Conquest 24
  motte 17
Northern Premier League...137
Northwich Bridge 17,25
  Building Society 115
  Constituency 101
  Gas Co 43
  Manor 23,25,27,42,75
  Pond 42,58
  Regatta 137
  RDC *4*,127,129
  Station 66
  town centre 15
  UDC *4*,41,42,75,103,129,
    153
  Victoria ... 136,137,*139*,*140*
NSPCC 44,74
nuclear research 150
Oakleigh 19
Okell, George 53
Oulton Park 127
Over, Mayor of 43
Owley Wood 129
pack horses 59
Padua University 90
Page, Mr 52
Parks, Joseph 43
Parr's Bank 89
Pavilion Theatre 136,*142*
Peckforton Castle 38,127
Penrhyn, Lord 37,39
  henhouse *39*
Perrin, Michael 150
Pettypool 90
Pickering's Wharf 55
Pickmere Randle 24
pit ponies 113
plague 29
Plumley 28
police *49*,*100*
Polish refugees 150
polythene 150
Post Office 113
pottery kiln 19,20
Port Sunlight 128,149
Preston Brook 56
protective clothing 97
Quorn Hunt 135
railways *152*
Rayner, Marjorie 138
rate demand, 1849 .... *111*
Reading Rooms 74
Red Cross Hospital 148
Reformation 28
Regal Cinema 136
Revenue men 38,127
Richard III 27
Rifle Volunteers 134
Rimming House 27
river carnival 137
Roaring Men 113

157

Roberts Bakery *147*
Robinson, Isaac 104
rock salt 13
Roe, James 73
Roman Black Country 18
   burials 14
   forts *16,17,18,20*
   helmet *16*
   roads 17,19,*19*,23
Romantic Movement 114,
                                      130
Rowing Club 137
Royal Society 90,102
Rudheath 25,28,38,91,95,
                                127,129
Ruloe 135
Runcorn 57,81,95,101
Rupert, Prince 32
Ruskin, John 41,74
Rustic Mystic 54
St Helen's 24,80
Saltaire 128
salt arches 104,*106*
   barrows 42,85
   killers of 28
   mines 86,*112*,113
   Museum ... 13,18,24,43,103
   officials 18
   pans 18,19,*20,21*,24,35,
                                      82,94
   pits 18,28
   smugglers 38
   taxes 24,38,127
   Union 80,81,95,103,104,
                                         114
   viewers 28
   works .... 79 *et seq*,81,*82,83,*
                            84,85,153
Saltersford 23,*25*,26
   Lock 81
Salterswall 23
Salvation Army 53,139
Samian ware 19
Sandbach 58
Sandifords 80
Sandiway 13,32,44,90,135
   Manor 130
Saner, Col John 57
Sankey Brook Canal 56
Saxons 23
schools etc
   (A1)lostock 74,136
   Barnton Brunner 78
   Dame 75
   Castle Girls' 75
   Catholic 75
   Girls' High 76
   Gt Budworth Grammar...73
   Hartford 76
   Leftwich 76
   Miss Bell's Academy *39*
   National 74
   Northwich 73
   Runcorn 74
   St Paul's, Danesbridge .. 75
   Stedman College 136
   Sunday Schools . 52,74,139
   Verdin Technical
      College 100,103,*106*,
                              127,137
   Victoria Road 75
   Wesleyan 74
   Winnington 76,*133*
   Hall Seminary 75

Winsford 74
Witton Boys' 75
   Grammar *22*.31,33,
                            73,74,76,77
Shakespeare, Wm 27,73
Shopping Centre 43,116
Ship Canal 81
Showman's Guild 136
Silvertown 91
sluices 60
slum clearance 130
Slyford, Thomas 55
Smith Barry, Hon John . 135
Society of Chemical
   Industry 90
soda ash 89
Solvay, Ernest 89,90
soulcaking 139
Sowerby 51
Spotswood, Capt 31
Stalbridge, Lord 37
State Theatre *142*
Stanley, Earls of Derby ... 27
   Lord 89
   of Alderley 38
streets, roads etc
   Albion Way 102
   Appleton Street 128
   Avenue, the 121
   Bakehouse Street 27
   Boundary Street 27
   Castle Hill *19*,136
   Chester Road 129
   Church Road 138
   Walk 75
   Clay Pipe Alley 44
   Cockpit Lane 135
   Crown Street 41,51
   Crum Hill 27,126,128
   Daleford's Lane 53
   Dock Road 60
   Dyar Terrace 129,*133*
   Greenall's Road 128
   Golden Square 73,127
   Highfield Hill 32
   High Street 27,43,*105*,
                                     116
   Hollow Way 18
   Jubilee Street 117
   King Street 18,*19*
   Leicester Street 42,53,
                                126,136
   Lock Street 52,135
   London Road ... 55,74,103,
                          116,*124*,127
   Manchester Road 127
   Moreton Street 128
   Moss Road 90
   Navigation Road 44,*64*,
                                 94,128
   New Warrington Road...136
   New Street 37,41,*49*,127
   Paradise Street 127
   Park Street 127
   Penny's Lane 55
   Pleasant Street 127
   Queens Street 44
   Rathbone Place 127
   Schoolmaster's Lane 73
   Sheath Street 27
   Ship Hill 43
   Solvay Road 102,128
   Station Road 44
   Temperance Terrace .. 128

Timber Lane 41,53,74,
                                  75,*131*
Town Row 27
Twemlow Place 127
Warrington Road 80
Waterloo Road 18,19,
                            127,128,*131*
Weaver Street 17
   plaque 64
Witton Street 3,10,13,
                 23,24,43,44,53,74
Yates Court 44
York Street 27
Stubbs, Albert 151
   Katherine 32
'Stumpers'136,*142*
subsidence ... 70,*112,118,119*,
                                    138
   compensation 115
Sugden, Samuel 52
Sutton, John 73
swimming 136,137,*145*
Sydney Harbour Bridge...43
Tangye, Albert 91
Tarporley 135
terminating building
   societies 128
Theatre Court 52
Thompson, Jabez 127
   family 103
Thorley, Samuel 55
timber-framed buidings . 114,
                                     122
Thorn Cottage 74
Times, the 95,101
Tin Town 129, *132*
Tollema(r)che, John .. 38,127
Touche, Rose la 75
Town Bridge(s) 25,27,31,
                 32,67,68,69,136,137
   Hall 136
Townsend, Gp Capt 91
Townshend, Squire Lee . 135
Trafford, Cecil de 103
Trent & Mersey Canal 37
Triassic 13
Tsar, the 80
Turnpike Trusts 55
Turning Point *151*
Twambrooks 24
Twemlow, John 127
Tythe map 74
United Alkali Co 149
Usher, Archbishop 31
Urban District Council ... 41,
                            42,103,129
Vale Royal 23,27,28,32,
                                  36,137
   Abbey 73,*108*
   Borough Council ... 81,153
   Cut 60
Venables of Kinderton 18,
                                   24,38
Verdin Baths *107*
   Sir Joseph . 94,101,102,*109*
   Park 17,115,137,138
   Robert 101,102,*107*
   Sir Thomas 73
   Sir William H. 101,102
Vernon family 38
Vernacular Revival .. 115,*121*
Viaduct 65
Vicarsway Park 42
Victoria Bridge 57,68,70

Club 138
   Infirmary 103
   Queen 51,90,101
Victory Memorial Hall ... 138
Wade Brook(es) 24,42,79
wakes 136
walking days 139
Wallers 28
Wallerscote..19,23,25,*124*,150
Ward Flats 61
   Thomas 103
Warburton, Col Hugh 37
   Sir George 55
   Lady 55
   Peter 28,135
   Rowland Everton 130
Warrington 90,95
   Museum 19
wash house 46
Waterlow, Sir Sidney 114
water supply 42
Watling Street Chambers...115
Watt, James 35
Weaver Locks 60
   flats 94
   Navigation 43,44,53,56,
                                 57,*111*
   River 13,14,25,28,36,55,
              81,102,114,115,136,137
   towpath 93
   Trustees 74
   Valley 89
Weaverham 19,32,129
Webb, William 36
Weber, Orlando 149
Wedgewood, Josiah 56
Wesley, John 51,52,53
Westminster, Duchess of....*100*
Weston Point 81
White, Charles 53
Whitegate 130
Whitehall 129
White Mischief 103
white slaves 95,101
Whittle, Frank 157
Widnes 81,89,95
Wilderspool 18
Williams, Leader 60
Wilson, Rev Job 51
Wincham 28,44,56,81,137,
                                     151
   Hall 135
Winnington .. 25,28,31,36,37,
       41,42,51,90,94,128,129,
                                133,137
   Bank House 103
   Battle of 32
   Bridge *34*
   Co-operative Soc 129
   family 28
   Hall (Club) 21,90,102,
                        104,136,138
   Estate 89
   Orangery 39
   Seminary 41
   Swing Bridge 70,81
   Wharf 62
Winsford 41,55,56,57,79,
       89,93,95,101,102,150
Witton cum Twambrooks . 24,
       28,41,42,51,114,130
Witton Albion ... 136,*140*,141
   Brook 36,56
   Cemetery 54

Manor 42	Woolfe, Gen 74	Wyatt, Samuel 37	Yarwoods 115,150
Rock Salt Mine 112	women workers 96	Wyman, Jane 90	Yates, William 44
Wood, Canon Maitland .. 130	World War I ... 58,90,97,104,	Wynington, Richard 44	York Minster 91
workhouse 41,42,93,*111*	*148*	Wynsford by Vale Royal	Yorkshire Buildings .. 41,127
Worsley, Katherine 91	II 44,129,138,150	Council 130	

ENDPAPERS (FRONT) LEFT: Northwich c1600; RIGHT: Vernon Estate map of 1721. (BACK) LEFT & CENTRE: the 1828 sale of Witton cum Twambrookes; RIGHT: Northwich in 1890.

Subscribers

Presentation Copies

1 Northwich Town Council
2 Vale Royal Borough Council
3 Cheshire County Council
4 Northwich Library
5 *Northwich Chronicle*
6 Dialysis Unit, Withington Hospital
7 County Councillor Ron Carey

8 Brian Curzon
9 Clive & Carolyn Birch
10 F. Kettle
11 Joan Glazebrook
12 B.W.M. Jaques
13 Alan Spence
14 Eric Southern
15 Marjorie Afzal
16 Charles Ellison
17 T. Collins
18 Geoffrey Jackson
19 G.W. Jordan
20 H. Patterson
21 Nichola Margaret Humphreys
22 B.A. Jackson
23 Harry Winstanley
24 D.E. Brown
25 J. Riches
26 Nigel Graeme Cope
27 Bryan Dearden
28 Nick Hughes
29 Mrs F.Z. Davies
30 Mrs L. Burrows
31 Carol Forrester Inwood
32 E. Stock
33 Mrs J. McLoughlin
34 A. Dutton
35 R.W. Deakin
36 Mrs R. Martin
37-38 K. Duncalf
39 Victoria & Albert Museum
40 Guildhall Library, City of London
41 Jean Elizabeth Griffiths
42 Mrs M. Bromidge
43 Sue Roberts
44 M.J. Jennings
45 Mrs K. W. Hall
46 Mrs J. Carson
47 Margaret Clarke
48 Kevin Smith
49 A.R. Hurley
50 Barton County Junior School
51 Mrs K. Doeser
52 Heather Joy Hills
53 Cuddington C.P. School
54 Mrs D.M. Chantler
55 W.J. Eastaway
56 Mrs J.E. Maxted
57 Mrs D.M. Chantler
58 F.G. Robinson
59-60 St Nicholas High School
61 Mrs J. Tyson
62 Mrs Pat Gayton
63-64 Mrs M.R. Green
65 Marion Newby
66 Mrs Helen J. Green
67 Barton Pharmacy

68-69 Magpie Antiques
70-71 Weaverham High School
72 Councillor Kevin P. Mannion
73 Janet Nattrass
74 S.L. Watson
75 Paul Lavell
76 S. Gillett
77 J.M. Eardley
78 P.J. Shufflebottom
79 John Anthony Curzon
80-83 Hartford Manor C.P. School
84 Alan James O'Brien
85 Mrs J. Lyon
86 G.H. Wilson
87 Mrs Sandra Crocker
88 Arthur Stelfox
89 Mrs L. Boylan
90 B.R. Rivers
91 Mrs. M. Wade
92 Mrs D. Tomkinson
93 J. Edwards
94 Mr & Mrs R. Sage
95 Mrs M. Edgerley
96 R. Lambert
97 Thomas A. Wilding
98 Andrew M. Adams
99 R.S. Riley
100 A.N. Johnson
101 J. M. Hindley
102 Pauline F. Little
103 N. Curbishley
104 Mrs G. Withenshaw
105 Miss H.J. Smallwood
106 Mrs J.F.M. Anderson
107 Royston Kalsalt
108-109 B. Woodward
110 Miss M. Sinclair
111 J. Southern
112 Mrs L.E. Hartley
113 S.E. Cleal
114 M.A. Grimes
115 G.F. Watts
116 Mrs B. Sandbach
117 Margaret Cunliffe
118 W. Harris

119 C.M. Robinson
120 Terry Dodd
121 John Geoffrey & Heather Sharps
122-131 Cheshire Record Office
132 J.A. Edge
133 Mr & Mrs R.V. Birdsey
134 Anon
135 Mr Spencer
136 Brian Dale
137 A.R. Littler
138 Mrs M. Poole
139 J.H. Jackson
140 S. Platt
141 K.R. Edwards
142 John Prest
143 J. Boothman
144-145 Mr & Mrs Aycliffe
146 John Senior
147 C.S. Plant
148 J.K. Cross
149 Christine Kirk
150 H. Buckley
151 Eugene Murray-Golding
152 Mrs C. Ball
153 Mrs A.R. Cash
154 John Platt
155 A. Blake
156 Jean Walton
157 D.L. Patch
158 E.M. Hawes
159 J.K. Cross
160 Mr Anderson
161 Dr K.H. Bray
162 I.M. Voinus
163 B.D. Broadhurst
164 Robert Iskem
165 E.M. Hawes
166 D. Johnson
167 A. Curzon
168 S. Platt
169-188 Cheshire Libraries
189 A.B. Dale
190 Arthur A. Carter
191 Paul Taylor
192 George Majewicz
193 C. Beckett

194 Mr & Mrs J.C. Hodgkinson
195 Doris Hamlett-Bushby
196 J.S. Edgley
197 Sandiway C.P. School
198 Tina Wright
199 Peter Wharmby
200 Sheila Deighton
201 M. Murphy
202 James Conboy
203 Mrs B. Duncan
204 Mrs M. Wright
205 New Cheshire Salt Works Ltd
206 Audrey Grimsditch
207 Northwich Town Council
208 D.F. Drewitt
209 Joan Shipton
210 M. Garnett
211 L. McCulloch
212 FHS of Cheshire
213 Granville Boardman
214 Harry Naylor
215 Florence Eve Martin
216 I.C.I. PLC
217 R. Blann
218 K. Gill
219 Stan Hancock
220 B. Glaze
221 J. Williams
222 Norman & Mary Barber
223 Irene Popplestone
224 Peter John Lowthion
225 Mr & Mrs W. Beevers
226 Gladys N. Brown
227 Arthur Kirkham
228 Peter Kirkham
229 M. Smallcross
230 Geoffrey Knowles Painter
231 Olive Read
232 M. Gorrill
233 P. Woolrich
234 B.G.C. Salisbury
235 Mark Burdon
236 P. Buckley
237 P.J. Craven
238 Sheila Mary Cranmer-Gordon
239 C. Ravenscroft
240 M.J. Leigh
241 George Ramsey Taylor
242 J.H. Gorst
243-244 Manchester Public Libraries
245 Allan D. Konca
246 Ada F. Gleave
247 A. Buckley
248 P. Wharmby
249 Denise Venables
250 Ruth Worsley Mackenzie
251 Beryl Duncan
252 B.J. Shufflebottom
253 T.J. Duffy
254 S.E. Whalley

Remaining names unlisted.

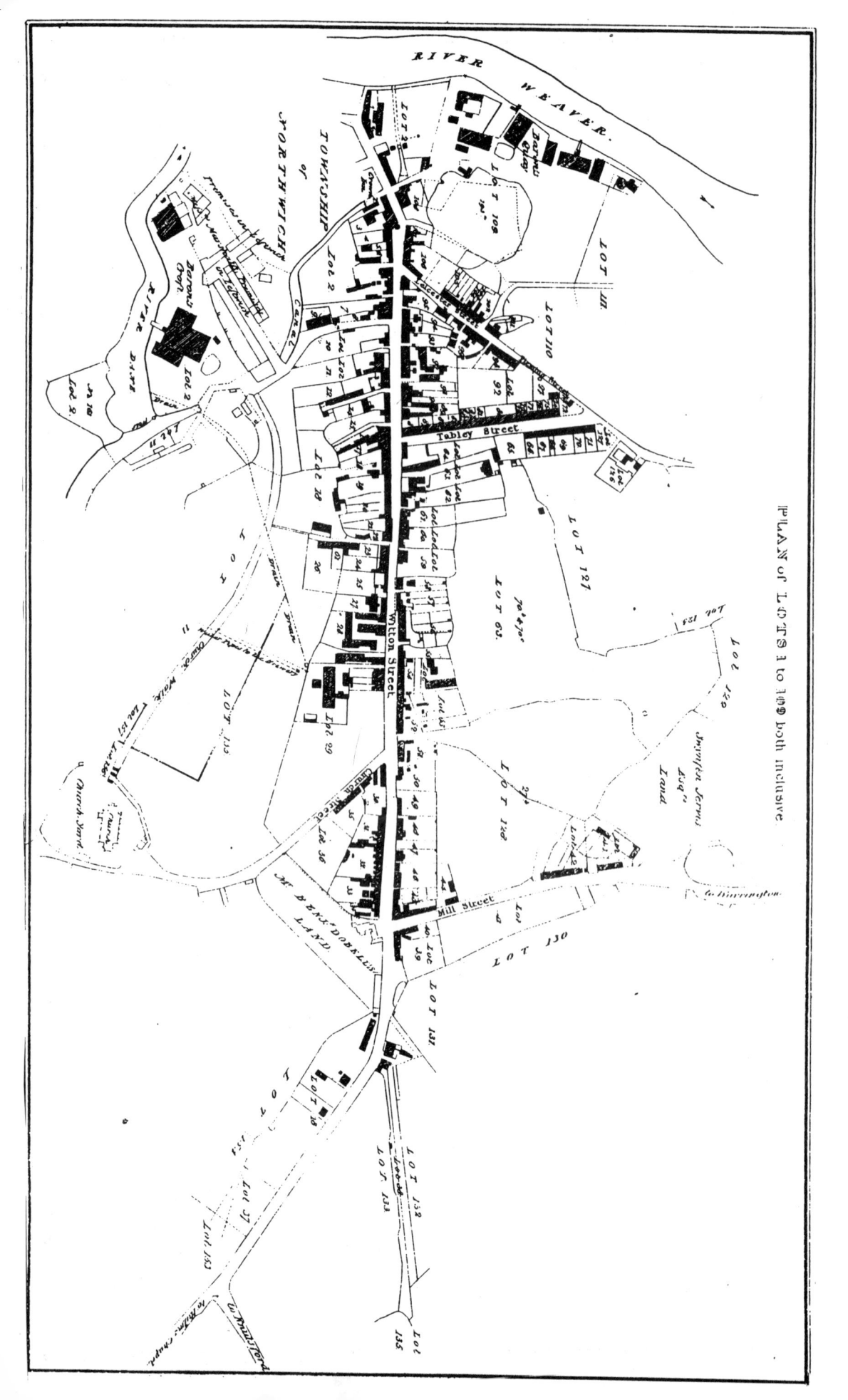

In Chancery.

Between THOMAS LIS...
The Right Hono...
now GEORG...

MANOR

AD...

WITTON CU...

Several PEWS in ...

TOGE...

Freeh...

Rich Meadow, Pasture, A...
Rock Salt Mines, Quays...
of Water, a...

IN T...

Witton Cum Twambr...

COUNT...

500 STATUT...

Part of the Estates late of the Right Ho...

Which w...

Pursuant to ...

With the Approbation of ...
The Master to ...

CROWN IN...

IN THE

On MONDAY the 29...

AND FIV...

The Sale to commence at E...

Printed Particulars and Conditions of Sale may be ha... at the ...
NANT, HARRISON, and TENNANT, 8, Gray's Inn Squa...
Knutsford, and Messrs. BURN and SON, Land Surveyors...
to shew the respective Lots); and at the PLACE OF SA...

J. Williams,